# THE LITTLE
# BOOK OF
# MARMALADE

## LUCY DEEDES

*An imprint of HarperCollinsPublishers Ltd.*

HQ

An imprint of HarperCollinsPublishers Ltd.

1 London Bridge Street

London SE1 9GF

This paperback edition 2020

1

First published in Great Britain by

HQ, an imprint of HarperCollinsPublishers Ltd. 2020

Copyright © Lucy Deedes

illustrations: ©Alenka Karabanova /Shutterstock

Book Design: Steve Wells

Lucy Deedes asserts the moral right to be

identified as the author of this work

A catalogue record for this book is

available from the British Library

ISBN: 978-0-00-837845-5

Printed and bound by RRD in China

# CONTENTS

# WINTER

# SPRING

# SUMMER

# AUTUMN

# INTRODUCTION

**L**ike many of us, I learned to cook by 'helping' my mother, or rather by sitting on the dented lid of the Aga reading aloud to her while she worked. The kitchen was the warmest place to be and there were plums and bullaces to be bottled, bread to be made and butter to be churned. Orphaned lambs snuggled up to the stove and the Jack Russell terriers mooched about picking up crumbs. When Seville oranges arrived in the shops for those few weeks in January, my mother usually froze them whole so that she could make marmalade later on when she had time. There was too much to do in those short winter days when the sheep were lambing, the ponies were in stables and the Jersey cows' trough was freezing over. I don't think she actively taught me to cook but I must have absorbed something in between the pages of *The Code of the Woosters*.

Marmalade was historically – and should still be – regarded as a luxury food. It was made from expensive imported items and treated with all the reverence it deserves. It has been with us for hundreds of years in one form or another – as a Portuguese sweetmeat, an after-dinner digestif, as a rich quince slab to be cut into squares like Turkish delight, an aphrodisiac – before it turned into the most famous breakfast ingredient ever. And it has been a breakfast necessity for over 200 years for everyone from the Queen (who reputedly has Tiptree Orange Marmalade on her white breakfast toast) to James Bond; every well-run household from the reign of Queen Victoria onwards has made sure the larder was well-stocked with homemade marmalade.

We all know the sort of marmalade we like just as we know how we like our coffee. Some people like a clear jelly, with just a few wafers of peel hanging like seahorses in the jar; some a firm orange mixture with no extras. Some refuse to touch it unless it's a dark, raffish paste, boiled down almost to toffee with a passing suggestion of booze about it.

Part of the appeal of marmalade is its mysterious marriage between sweet and bitter; finding that balance is certainly what makes it so rewarding to make and also why it gives such a kick to almost anything to which you add it.

Some regular marmalade makers stick to the tried-

and-tested Grandmother's Recipe: The Receipt Book, a precious document with sticky pages, fearing that if they go off-piste and introduce an exotic new ingredient it will all go terribly wrong.

Embarking on marmalade-making for the first time can be unnerving, but it is not difficult: it is after all a combination of just three ingredients: citrus fruit, sugar and water. Having said that, there are important steps to follow and it can occasionally surprise you and refuse to cooperate. Even now, I find that sometimes the rolling, hissing boil doesn't happen. (What! No rolling boil?) It skips that bit, as a joke. Or you would swear it was ready, but then it won't set in the jars. (Relax, leave it overnight.)

I had a few years of ill health when much was out of my control, and that was when I started to appreciate how soothing it is to make marmalade, how very satisfying to produce something good to look at and good to eat, which almost everyone is delighted to receive as a present. Perhaps there was a subconscious vote of confidence for the future in preserving fruit and storing it for later; I didn't know T.E. Lawrence's 'Happiness is a by-product of absorption' then, but there is a sense of peace and contentment that descends when you have an absorbing physical task to do. Homemade marmalade is 'slow', not fast food, and it takes a bit of concentration, but the results are worth the effort.

You may want to make enough in January to last you for the whole year; or you might prefer to make a few jars here and there, throughout the year, using a handful of frozen oranges or experimenting with other citrus fruit like limes and grapefruit, and adding herbs, like thyme or rosemary in the summer, lavender flowers or ginger in July. Cloves and warming spices are delicious in a pre-Christmas batch. I personally think that the exciting sharpness of marmalade is at its very best when the marmalade is fresh, but however long you keep it before you eat it, the most gratifying thing is that every jar you make will be uniquely your own.

The recipes in this book are my own, handed down from my mother and many generous and accomplished cooks, as well as borrowed favourites from friends. They've been tried and tested over the years, and tinkered with along the way to suit more modern tastes. Methods vary slightly from one recipe to another, but isn't that the beauty of home cooking? I hope you enjoy making marmalade whatever the season, and that you find your favourite among the many in this special collection.

# HANDY TIPS BEFORE YOU BEGIN

## A FEW CLUES

1. Buy organic, unwaxed citrus fruit if you can because you are eating the whole fruit, and non-organic fruit will have been well doused with sprays. Ask your greengrocer. Discard any dodgy-looking or bruised fruit.

2. Use fresh or frozen oranges. Seville oranges freeze brilliantly, but freezing does weaken the pectin over time so it's a good idea to add fresh citrus fruit – lemons, grapefruit, limes – when you're cooking with frozen oranges.

3. Use granulated or caster sugar, or soft dark sugar for a more deeply coloured marmalade (or try preserving sugar as I do; it gives the clearest appearance). Use brown sugar only if you want a darker, stickier marmalade.

4. Make sure your jars and lids are sparkling clean (see page 9 for how to sterilise).

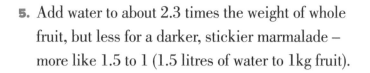

5. Add water to about 2.3 times the weight of whole fruit, but less for a darker, stickier marmalade – more like 1.5 to 1 (1.5 litres of water to 1kg fruit).

6. Work to the ratio of 4:3 cooked pulp to sugar, and 2:1 for dark, bitter marmalade as it contains treacle (otherwise it would be far too sweet), but by all means go for 1:1 should you wish. Play with the levels if you want less or more sugar.

7. Use a sugar thermometer to test for setting point: it is ready when it reaches 105°C. You will soon get to know what the marmalade looks and sounds like when it's ready – by the seething noise of a rolling boil and the way the marmalade hangs on the spoon like icicles when it's nearly done. Otherwise, use the wrinkle test (see page 9).

8. It's very important to leave the marmalade to settle before you pour it into the warm jars: the mixture needs to congeal slightly so that the peel is held suspended in the jelly. If you pot up too fast, the peel will swim up to the top of the jar. And I always use a scalded plastic or Pyrex jug to pot up the marmalade; it makes less mess than a ladle.

9. Fill the jars to the very top, but not so it will touch the lids, and don't bother with waxed paper discs – you don't need them with screw-top lids.

10. Store in a cool and dark place, and keep in the fridge once opened.

## USING AN ELECTRIC JUICER

Not only is it quicker and easier, but an electric juicer will strip off all the membranes as it juices, leaving just the pith behind. If you are juicing by hand, you will need to tug off these membranes to add to the muslin bag.

## SOAKING THE FRUIT

If time allows, it is a good idea to soak the chopped oranges and the muslin bag of pips overnight because the all-important pectin which will set your marmalade is in the skin and pips, not the orange juice and flesh, and a long soak will thoroughly extract it. It will also soften the tough skins and reduce cooking time. I also always leave the cooked fruit to soak overnight or for a few hours to draw out all the possible pectin. But if you don't have the time, then just crack on without soaking.

### STERILISING JARS AND LIDS

Put the jars and lids through a
hot dishwasher cycle and then onto
a baking tray in a 150°C/130°C fan/Gas 2 oven
(jars for 15 minutes, lids for 5) once the marmalade
reaches 102°C–103°C, so they're still warm when you
fill them.

### THE WRINKLE TEST

The traditional way of testing for a set is to leave
a saucer or ramekin in the fridge to get cold, put a
spoonful of marmalade on it, leave for a minute and
see if it wrinkles when you push your finger through it.
Remove the marmalade from the heat while you do this,
and replace on the heat if it's not yet done, repeating the
process until it reaches setting point.

### SEALING THE JARS

Put the lids on immediately the jar is filled but only
loosely. Return the jars to the 150°C/130°C fan/Gas 2
oven for 5 minutes and then tighten the lids for a good
seal before leaving to cool.

WINTER

**W**inter is usually a time for hibernation. As the nights draw in and the temperature drops, there's nothing better than to cosy up at home. So it's the perfect opportunity to work some marmalade magic in the kitchen. Marmalade in winter is like nothing else. Seville oranges from Spain are harvested from November onwards and they're sometimes available before Christmas to make the perfect sticky glaze to any Christmas centrepiece.

DECEMBER

# MARMALADE WITH HONEY (NO SUGAR)

This is worth a try if you want to be sugar-free. You don't get the set, and the finished result is more of a compote than a jelly, but it has a very good, fresh taste.

Makes 2 small jars

**1 Seville orange**
**1 clementine or mandarin**
**3 large sweet oranges**
**2 tbsp good-quality honey**

Peel the Seville orange, clementine or mandarin and one of the sweet oranges. Break the fruit into segments, removing the pips and as much of the white pith as you can. Whizz the fruit pieces to a purée in a food processor.

Shave off any excess pith on the inside of the peels and slice or chop the peel finely. Put the pips, membranes and excess pith in a muslin bag and tie a knot in the top.

Juice the remaining 2 oranges and add the juice to a preserving pan with the fruit purée, the sliced peel and the muslin bag. Cook on a low heat for about 10–15 minutes until the peel is soft.

Add the honey, stir it in and simmer for another 10 minutes until the mixture has reduced. Test for taste – don't burn your mouth – and add a little more honey if needed.

Pot into sterilised and warm jars and leave to cool. You can then keep in the fridge.

# REDUCED-SUGAR MARMALADE

**I** am often asked for a lower sugar marmalade. I wanted to see if reducing the sugar from the 4:3 cooked pulp to sugar ratio to 4:2 would affect the set; it doesn't, and I don't find it noticeably less sweet.

Makes 5–6 x 450g jars

1 lemon, plus the juice of 2 more
2 white grapefruit (about 600g)
3 Seville oranges (about 420g)
1 lime
1 bay leaf
About 2.7 litres water
About 1.1kg granulated or preserving sugar

Weigh the lemon with the rest of the fruit and note down the total weight. Wash and chop the fruit as directed on page 32 and slice into shreds according to how you like it, reserving the pips, orange membranes and any excess pith in a muslin bag. Put the fruit shreds into a pan with the bay leaf. Weigh out 2.3 times water to the weight of the whole fruit and add to the pan. Leave to soak overnight.

The next day, bring to the boil and simmer for about 2 hours, until soft. Remove from the heat and leave for another 24 hours, if possible.

Remove the bay leaf and measure the volume of pulp. For each 100ml of pulp, add 50g sugar and add to the pan with the lemon juice. Stir over a low heat until the sugar is dissolved.

Turn up to full heat and boil fast until it reaches setting point, at 105°C, or use the wrinkle test (see page 9).

Remove from the heat and leave to settle for 15–20 minutes. Pot into sterilised and warm jars, seal and leave to cool (see page 9).

## CHILDHOOD MEMORIES

My parents kept bees at home and the jars of honey were labelled RAPE, since the bees mostly fed on yellow rape flowers. One year when we went on holiday to Suffolk, a colleague of my father's brought her family to stay in the house, and in our absence her teenage son humorously marked the other jars in the cupboard PILLAGE, MURDER, INCEST and ARSON.

# MARMALADE RUM SOUR COCKTAIL

Serves 1

**60ml dark rum**
**1/3 egg white**
**Splash of sugar syrup**
**Juice of 1 lime**
**1 tsp marmalade**

Shake all the ingredients in a Boston shaker and strain into a chilled cocktail or sour glass.

**W**hen I started making marmalade thirty years ago, I used old jam jars and recycled lids. It was just for the family, so the sterilisation methods may have been a bit slapdash; sometimes I bottled it up too soon and the peel rushed to the top of the jar like fish in a feeding frenzy. I put paper discs inside the lid – no idea why, but my mother had done that. If I took a jar to my hostess, I peeped inside to check there was no mould.

Once I had decided to enter some marmalade for the Dalemain competition in 2014, I knew I needed to up my game, because the judging is rigorous and any careless errors will be Found Out. No pips lurking in the jar; no air bubbles; evenly chopped peel suspended throughout the jar. Next, I decided to sell my marmalade in local farmers' markets and things went up a notch again. I did my cooking swathed in chef's whites like an Egyptian mummy, topped with a pink bath cap, bought a thermometer to take the guesswork out of the all-important setting point, and prepared myself for the inspection by the local council. I gave the dog away, cleaned the kitchen so it shone like an operating theatre and bought a chef's hat from the Sandringham gift shop, with BUCKINGHAM PALACE on it. All went well, the inspector merely suggesting the addition of a pedal bin. Only joking, the dog went to play with a friend.

Then there was the paperwork – temperature levels, pH levels, sterilisation records, sell-by dates. Silicon spoons to avoid those curry-flavoured wooden spoons. Labels designed, frowned at and redesigned by my children. An extra chest freezer so I could store enough Seville oranges for a year. Still it goes on. A market customer might ask me, Do you make a low-sugar one? No sugar? One with whisky? All suggestions and the opportunity to try something new are much welcomed.

# LAMBS' LIVER WITH ORANGE

Serves 4

**350g fresh lambs' liver (or calves' if you prefer)**
**25g plain flour**
**2 tbsp olive oil, plus more if needed**
**4 rashers of streaky bacon, roughly chopped**
**1 onion, sliced**
**Grated zest and juice of 1 orange**
**1 tsp fresh rosemary, chopped, or dried**
**1 small glass of red wine**
**Salt and freshly ground black pepper**

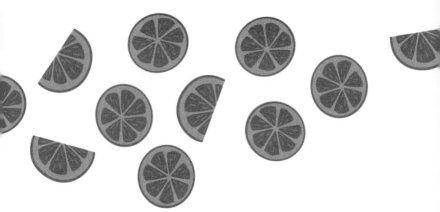

Place the liver in a bowl of salted water and leave for at least 30 minutes, then dry with kitchen paper and trim off everything you don't like the look of, to give you smooth pieces with no lumps or bumps. Liver is not expensive and we can afford to be fussy with it.

Spread the flour on a plate, season with salt and pepper and roll the liver pieces in the flour.

Heat the oil in a flameproof casserole or saucepan, add the bacon and fry until it has released its fat and started to take on a little colour, then add the onion and cook until soft but not browned. Add the pieces of liver, and more oil if necessary, and cook gently for about 5 minutes. Add the orange zest and juice, the rosemary and the wine, and allow the alcohol to cook off.

Turn the heat down low, cover and allow to simmer for about 25 minutes, topping up with liquid if needed.

Serve with mashed potatoes or brown rice and some greens.

# ORANGE DRIZZLE CAKE

Serves 10

2 oranges
200g butter, at room temperature
200g golden caster sugar
3 large eggs, beaten
200g self-raising flour
40g ground almonds
1 tsp fresh rosemary, chopped
1 large tbsp marmalade, shreds roughly chopped

**For the drizzle**
4 tbsp caster sugar
2 tbsp water

Heat the oven to 180°C/160°C fan/Gas 4. Grease a 20cm cake tin and line with baking parchment.

Slice 1 of the oranges into rounds and lay the the slices neatly in a single layer to cover the base of the prepared tin.

Cream the butter and sugar together in a food mixer. Mix in the beaten egg a third at a time, adding a spoonful of the flour if it looks like curdling. Sift in the flour and ground almonds and mix until smooth. Grate in the zest of the remaining orange and add a squeeze of the juice (keep the rest of the juice for the drizzle). Stir in the rosemary and marmalade.

Spoon the mixture into the cake tin, being careful not to dislodge the orange slices. Bake for 30–45 minutes, until a skewer inserted into the middle comes out clean, then remove from the oven and allow to cool in its tin for 15 minutes.

Meanwhile, to make the drizzle, mix the remaining orange juice with the sugar and water in a small pan. Warm over a medium heat, stirring as the liquid turns into a syrup.

Turn the cake out of its tin and onto a plate, prick holes on the top with a skewer, and pour over the syrup. Leave for a few minutes for the syrup to sink in. Serve warm as a pudding, with cream or ice cream. Once cold, eat as cake!

# CHOCOLATE AND MARMALADE TART

Serves 10

**For the pastry**
250g plain flour, plus extra for dusting
140g cold butter, diced
80g caster sugar
1 egg yolk, beaten

**For the filling**
3 heaped tbsp marmalade
85g butter
1 tsp orange extract
250g dark chocolate (70% cocoa solids),
  broken into small pieces
400ml double cream

**To decorate (optional)**
1 tbsp candied Seville orange peel (see page 68),
  chopped, or 1 tbsp hazelnuts, almonds
  or walnuts, chopped

To make the pastry, put the flour and butter into a food processor and process to a crumbly texture. Add the sugar and egg yolk and whizz briefly until the dough balls up. Wrap the pastry loosely in cling film and chill for at least 30 minutes.

Heat the oven to 180°C/160°C fan/Gas 4 and place a baking sheet near the top of the oven.

Roll out the pastry dough on a lightly floured surface to 3–4mm thick (about the thickness of a pound coin). Use to line a 24cm fluted, loose-bottomed tart tin, pushing the pastry well into the corners. Prick the bottom gently with a fork and leave the pastry a little higher at the edges, to trim later. Line the inside of the pastry case with baking parchment and fill with baking beans or rice, then ideally chill for 10 minutes.

Bake the pastry case on the baking sheet for 15 minutes, then gently lift out the parchment and beans and cook for a further 5 minutes until pale brown; leave to cool.

Separate out the marmalade peel from the syrup and chop it, then scatter it across the base of the cooled pastry case.

Melt the butter in a pan over a gentle heat, then add the chocolate, marmalade syrup and orange extract, and stir until melted and smooth. Heat the cream in a separate pan until almost boiling (do not bring to the boil as the mixture will split), then stir it into the chocolate mixture and keep stirring until smooth.

If needed, trim the top of the pastry case. Pour the chocolate filling into the pastry case and leave to cool and set completely. If you like, decorate with pieces of chopped candied orange or chopped nuts. Cut with a warm knife and serve with single cream.

The Sixties were not extravagant times, food-wise. On Christmas eve we might glance in our fridge and see nothing in there, except a turkey and possibly a ham, that would not have been there at any other time of year. It was the tradition and the quantity that mattered: having the same as we had last year and plenty of it.

My mother had green and organic leanings long before it was fashionable. When she bought a box of tangerines at Christmas, the soft blue tissue paper in which they were wrapped was carefully folded and placed in the downstairs cloakroom.

JANUARY

# SEVILLE ORANGE MARMALADE

If I am making this out of Seville orange season using frozen and defrosted oranges, then I add another lemon or two and perhaps a sweet orange to boost the pectin quantity. The ratio of water to fruit I use is 2.3:1 – 2.3 litres of cold water to 1 kg whole fruit. I have tinkered with sugar quantities over the years and my usual formula is now pulp to sugar: 4:3 (roughly translating as raw fruit to sugar: 3:4).

Soaking the chopped peel overnight is not essential if you are short of time, but it softens it, reducing the cooking time, and extracts the maximum possible pectin for a good set.

continued overleaf

Makes 5–6 x 450g jars

**1kg Seville oranges**
**250g lemons (2–3 lemons), plus the juice of 2 extra**
**2.8 litres water**
**1.7kg granulated or preserving sugar**

For most citrus fruit except Seville oranges, I quarter them and then cut the entire fruit into fine slices. Seville oranges are too full of pips for this, so halve and juice them, adding the juice to the pan and any membranes to the muslin. Cut the halved shells in half again and, if the white pith is very thick, shave some of it away by flattening out the piece of peel and running a knife along it – much as you would skin a fish fillet. Don't cut it all away; pith is vital to achieve a set and give that unique bitter taste to the marmalade. Add this pith to the muslin bag.

Cut the lemon quarters and orange peels into shreds about 2–4mm wide and add to the preserving pan with the water. Knot the muslin cloth and push it under the fruit and water. Ideally, leave to soak overnight.

The next day, bring the fruit and water to the boil and allow it to simmer gently for about 2 hours, stirring occasionally, pushing the bag under the water occasionally, until you can easily squash the peel with a wooden spoon. The water and fruit should be evenly mixed, like soup; if there is a clear band of water at the top then simmer it down some more. Remove from the heat, cover, and ideally leave it for another 24 hours.

Remove the muslin bag and place it in a sieve over a bowl to drain, squashing it gently to remove as much liquid as possible. Measure the volume of pulp from the pan (your pan may have measurements marked up the insides) and add sugar to a ratio of 4:3, so to each 100ml of pulp add 75g sugar. Add the lemon juice and the strained juice from the muslin to the pan.

Stir over a low heat until every grain of sugar has melted and you have a smooth, warm syrup. Turn the heat up high and switch on your oven to 150°C/130°C fan/ Gas 2. Once the marmalade is boiling, it will take at least 20 minutes to reach a set. Put a baking tray of clean jars, right way up, in the oven for 15 minutes to sterilise.

Stir the marmalade occasionally, watching the way the drips fall off the spoon, and when instead of dripping cleanly from the spoon, the drops join together and hang in strings, you are nearly there. Once the temperature reaches 105°C, take the pan off the heat and let it cool and settle for 15–20 minutes (or the peel may rise to the top of the jar when you pot it up). If you don't have a thermometer, use the wrinkle test (see page 9). Place your clean lids in the oven for 5 minutes.

Use the sterilising and sealing methods (see page 9). Screw the lids on loosely and return the full jars to the oven for 5 minutes, then use a tea towel to tighten the lids. Put them in a cool place, undisturbed, to cool before labelling.

# BUTTERFLIED LEG OF LAMB WITH SEVILLE ORANGE MARINADE

Serves 10–12

**2–2.5kg leg of lamb, butterflied**
**(ask your butcher to do this for you)**
**1 small sweet orange, sliced, to garnish**

**For the marinade**
**50g butter, melted**
**2 tbsp olive oil**
**2 tbsp ground cumin**
**Grated zest and juice of 1 Seville orange**
**1 heaped tsp chilli paste**
**1 small onion, chopped**
**2 garlic cloves, chopped**
**Salt and freshly ground black pepper**
**1 tbsp fresh thyme, chopped**
**1 tbsp fresh rosemary, chopped**

Mix the melted butter and oil together in a bowl and stir in the rest of the marinade ingredients, with salt and pepper to taste. Place the lamb in a shallow dish and spoon over the marinade. (Alternatively, use a large, sealable plastic bag to marinate the lamb, shaking it well.) Chill overnight. Remove from the fridge 1 hour before cooking.

Heat the oven to 180°C/160°C fan/Gas 4. Place the lamb in a roasting dish or tin and cover with the marinade.

Cook for about 1 hour or until a meat thermometer reads 60°C. Remove from the oven and leave to rest for 15 minutes.

Cut the lamb into slices, garnish with the sliced orange and serve with Greek yoghurt.

**Note**: You can cook the lamb on a barbecue, in which case give it about 5 minutes on each side on a high heat, then another 30 minutes or so over a lower heat, turning it a few times.

## MAUD'S SIMPLE
## SOURDOUGH LOAF

**M**y friend Maud, as well as being a sourdough whizz, collects beautiful old printed fabric which she makes into all sorts of things like bags, bath caps and eco food covering. She also prints her own designs onto remnant fabrics.

For a starter, clone a sourdough mother from a friend. Keep it in something like a bowl or large jam jar with holes in the lid, or loosely covered with greaseproof paper.

Makes 1 loaf

## Mother maintenance

You can keep the mother in the fridge to slow the fermentation down; if you do this, discard half of it every 3–5 days and feed with equal parts flour and water. If you go away, just feed it extra and don't worry – they are quite robust.

## Making a levain

The levain is the raising agent for your bread. Take your mother from the fridge the morning you want to mix your bread dough and put 1 tablespoon of it into a small bowl. Add 50g water and 50g flour, cover loosely and leave for about 5 hours. You will know it's ready when it is nice and bubbly.

## For the dough

**350g water**

**400g organic strong white flour**

**100g wholemeal rye, wheat or spelt, or a mixture**

**100g levain (see above)**

**9g sea salt**

About 2 hours before you go to bed, mix all the ingredients together in a bowl. Set aside to rest for 20 minutes.

Next comes kneading, which you do by stretching the dough over itself in the bowl. Do the stretching about 3–5 times before bed, every 20 minutes or so, covering the bowl with a plastic bag each time you leave it to rest. The dough should be feeling nice and elasticated.

continued overleaf

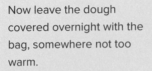

Now leave the dough covered overnight with the bag, somewhere not too warm.

In the morning the bowl will be full of bubbles. Pull the dough gently from the edge and fold into the middle, continue around the bowl until you have a neat package of dough ready to turn into a well-floured banneton. If you don't have one of these specialist proving baskets, you can use a bowl or colander lined with a linen tea towel and plenty of rice flour.

Prove for another 2 hours, or place in the fridge for 6–24 hours until you have time to cook it.

To cook your bread, heat the oven to 230°C/210°C fan/Gas 8 and place a large cast-iron enamel pot, such as a le Creuset, inside to heat up. When at full temperature, remove the pot, place a piece of baking parchment over the proving basket and turn it upside down over the pot. Gently lower the dough into the pot, using the parchment to help. Snip some lines into the surface of the dough with scissors, leaving the parchment where it is, put the lid on and place in the hot oven for 30 minutes, then take the lid off, turn the oven down to 200°C/180°C fan/ Gas 6 and cook for a further 10–20 minutes. Remove the bread from the pot and cool on a wire rack.

# ORANGE GIN

Makes about 1 litre

**4 Seville oranges**
**1 litre own-brand gin**
**1 bay leaf (optional)**
**100g caster sugar**
**100ml water**

You will need a large, clean lidded glass jar – Kilner or similar.

Using a swivel peeler, pare the zest from the oranges, then squeeze the juice of one of them. Pour the gin into the jar and add the zest strips and juice, and the bay leaf, if using. Seal and leave for anything from a few days to 2 weeks, shaking the jar each day.

Heat the sugar and water in a saucepan until the sugar is dissolved. Strain the infused gin to remove the zest and bay leaf, if you added one, then add the sweet syrup to the gin according to your taste.

Bottle, cork, drink.

In the 16ᵗʰ century, marmalade was one of Britain's most exotic and costly imports. Its name came from the Portuguese word for quince (marmelo): it was a rich, sticky paste of quinces, honey, nuts and rosewater, packed into round wooden boxes and embarking from southern Spain alongside a cargo of wine, pepper and olive oil (see page 44 for my recipe for something similar). In 1517 the tax paid on 50kg of marmalade was £350 at today's prices. It was valued by the wealthy, cut into squares and nibbled after dinner.

Picture the scene at Bristol docks, on 3rd January 1517; not yet Twelfth Night. Henry VIII is off spending Christmas with his first wife, Catherine of Aragon, at Greenwich Palace. A low fog hangs above the docks, with boats coming and going along the Bristol Channel. Some of them are off to Europe, carrying sensible British staples such as woollen cloth and hides. Some are coming from Ireland, bringing herrings and hake, and some from Bordeaux, with wine and Breton linen. But the cargoes on the Spanish and Portuguese ships are much more exciting.

The crew from the boat Christofur, from Bristol (master, Robert Avyntre) unload boxes and barrels onto the icy quay. These boats have to be nippy enough to dodge the Mediterranean pirates, and the Christofur has sailed from Sanlúcar de Barrameda in southern Spain, with its precious load of spiced quince paste.

Henry VIII was known to be partial to the paste, and there is a story of the court musician Mark Smeaton, who may or may not have been Anne Boleyn's lover, being discovered hiding in the cupboard where she kept her sweetmeats and marmalades, so it seems he was guilty of something.

Marmalade was for many years a generic term for any of these preserved fruit confections (cherry, pear, orange) and the first written recipe for the sort of marmalde we would recognise was Eliza Cholmondeley's in 1677. Early orange marmalades used little or no water and the end result was a stiff, solid paste that must have looked like ancient chutney. Fifty years or so later, Mary Kettilby added lemons to her recipe to allow the mixture to set sooner, so that marmalade threw off its stodgy image and became a lighter, clearer jelly more akin to the marmalade we know today.

# PAPPARDELLE WITH PROSCIUTTO AND SEVILLE ORANGES

Serves 4

500g fresh pappardelle or fettuccine (or 350g dried)
55g unsalted butter
80g prosciutto or serrano ham, torn into strips
Grated zest and juice of 1 (preferably Seville) orange
120ml double cream
25g freshly grated Parmesan
Salt and freshly ground black pepper

Bring a large pot of water to a boil. Season with plenty of salt, add the pasta and cook, stirring occasionally, until al dente.

While the pasta is cooking, melt the butter in a large frying pan over medium heat. Add the prosciutto and cook for a couple of minutes until browned.

Drain the pasta, reserving about 1 or 2 tbsp of the cooking water. Add the orange zest and juice, cream and reserved pasta water to the frying pan with the prosciutto. Add a good grinding of black pepper, bring to the boil then add the drained pasta and stir for a minute or so until well combined and heated through.

Sprinkle with the grated Parmesan and a couple of Basil leaves if you have them, serve with some dressed green leaves.

# TUDOR QUINCE MARMALADE

I thought I must try to make something similar to the original quince marmalades which were imported in such quantities into 16ᵗʰ-century Britain and prized by those who could afford them. I have sometimes, not very authentically, used pistachios instead of almonds. I failed to find beautiful Tudor round wooden boxes to pack it in.

Makes 30–35 squares

**2 large quince, peeled, cored and chopped**
**A few strips each of lemon and orange peel, excess pith scraped off, chopped**
**6 cardamom pods, bashed**
**A few slices of fresh ginger, peeled**
**A few pink peppercorns**
**About 375g granulated or preserving sugar**
**Juice of ½ lemon**
**Juice of ½ orange**
**50g dates, chopped**
**30g almonds, chopped**
**25g candied Seville orange peel**
**(see page 68 for homemade,**
**or use shop-bought)**
**1 tsp rosewater**

Put the quince, zests, cardamom, ginger and peppercorns into a large pan with enough water to cover. Bring to the boil then simmer for 40 minutes or until the quince is soft.

Remove the peppercorns, ginger and cardamom and whizz the fruit in a food processor.

Push the pulp through a mouli if you have one (skip this step if you don't) and measure the volume of this pulp. Transfer to a preserving pan.

For every 100ml of pulp, add 75g sugar to the pan. Add the lemon and orange juices. Boil the mixture until thick and bubbling volcanically, stirring occasionally to stop it sticking, and protecting your hand in case of hot spattering; it will turn red and smell quite delicious.

Take off the heat and mix in the dates, almonds, candied peel and rosewater; stir well. Spread the mixture into a glass or ceramic dish (about 22cm square) lined with greased parchment paper, so that the mixture is about 3–4cm deep.

Smooth the top and dry in a very cool oven, on a radiator or on the warm floor of the grill above the oven, for about 2 hours.

Cool, refrigerate and, when completely cold, turn out, remove the paper and cut into squares. It keeps well in the fridge wrapped in baking parchment.

**Note:** You could if you wanted dip half of each square into melted dark chocolate (70% cocoa solids), although that would be even less authentic than my recipe.

FEBRUARY

# DARK BITTER MARMALADE

This is a chunkier, slightly less sweet marmalade which contains four fruits and a spoonful of black treacle for a rich colour.

Makes about 5 x 450g jars

**500g Seville oranges (about 4), scrubbed**
**1 pink grapefruit**
**1 lime**
**2 lemons, plus the juice of 2 extra**
**About 1–1.5kg granulated or preserving sugar**
**1 tbsp black treacle**

Weigh all the whole fruit, make a note of the total weight and line a bowl with a piece of muslin.

Cut the oranges in half and juice them, collecting the pips and membranes in the muslin. Cut the orange halves in half again, then cut the peel into small squares, 1cm or less, shaving off some pith first if it's very thick and adding this to the muslin. Quarter and chop the other fruit and tip all the fruit and peel into a large preserving pan. Securely tie the muslin bag and add with the orange juice to the pan. Add 1.5 times water to the weight of fruit. (So for 850g fruit, add 1.275 litres water.) If you have forgotten to weigh the fruit, just add water to cover. Leave to soak overnight, if possible.

The next day, cover the pan lightly with foil and simmer for 1–2 hours until the peel is soft and can be cut with a wooden spoon. If possible, soak for another 24 hours, leaving the muslin bag in the fruit.

continued overleaf

Prepare about 5 clean jars and lids, turn the oven on to 150°C/130°C fan/Gas 2 and have a sugar thermometer ready (or a saucer in the fridge if you prefer) see page 9.

Remove the bag of pips and put in a sieve over a bowl to drain, squeezing it gently. Measure the volume of the marmalade mixture. I use 3 parts sugar to 5 parts pulp for this one, i.e. if there is 1500ml of pulp, add 900g of sugar, but you can use 4:5 if you prefer it sweeter. Add the lemon juice, sugar and black treacle, and stir over a very low heat until the sugar is totally dissolved.

Turn up the heat to full and boil the marmalade fast, stirring occasionally. It will take 30 minutes or more to reach setting point. When it reaches about 102°C, put the jars into the oven to sterilise for 15 minutes, adding the lids for the last 5 minutes.

When the marmalade reaches 105°C (or use the wrinkle test on page 9), take it off the heat. Let it stand for at least 15–20 minutes to allow the peel to settle before transferring to the warm jars, adding lids and sealing (see page 9).

# MARMALADE MOJITO

Serves 1

1 heaped tsp marmalade
2 tbsp dark rum
Juice of 1 sweet orange,
  plus an extra slice
1 star anise
Ice and tonic water, to serve

Put the marmalade, rum, orange juice and slice, and the star anise in a jar, screw on the lid and leave until ready to serve.

To finish, add some ice to the jar, screw the lid back on and shake well to mix and chill. Top up with tonic and serve.

**T**he world's largest and definitely most original marmalade festival takes place at Dalemain in Cumbria every March; run by the Hasell-McCosh family, its proceeds go to local hospice charities. Thousands of competitive cooks from the UK and overseas enter their marmalade and every jar is meticulously judged and scored: there are quirky classes including for octogenarians, for the military, for men and, interestingly, for bellringers.

Over the course of the festival weekend, the house and barn glow with thousands of jars of marmalade (each one with meticulous hand-written comments such as 'good set', 'jar not full to brim', 'pips' (oh the shame); piles of oranges and bowls of goldfish are reflected in mirrors and chandeliers so that the whole place is ablaze with sparkle. Paddington Bear

lumbers round in a stately fashion, smacking his lips; the sheep in the park are dyed orange, the Japanese ambassador's car is – obviously – orange. There is marmalade with gin, with matcha tea, with raspberries, with black garlic, tomatoes, chilli… you name it, they've put it in their marmalade.

The overall winner's marmalade is sold in Fortnum & Mason for a year, so it's definitely worth a go. There's no excuse for those competitive marmalade makers everywhere not to enter.

# ROAST PHEASANT WITH MARMALADE

Pheasant is lean and delicious and readily available during winter. If you're buying from a butcher, look for a plump one in good condition.

Serves 2 greedy people, or 4 with lots of side vegetables

**50ml rapeseed oil**

**20g butter**

**1 oven-ready pheasant**

**1–2 tbsp marmalade**

**Handful of thyme sprigs**

**1 glass of white wine**

**Sprinkling of plain flour**

**Salt and freshly ground black pepper**

**1 tbsp of single cream**

**For the bread sauce**

**140ml milk**

**1 small onion, halved**

**A few cloves**

**1 bay leaf**

**A few black peppercorns**

**2–3 tbsp breadcrumbs**

**A knob of butter**

Heat the oven to 190°C/170°C fan/Gas 5.

Heat the oil and butter in a flameproof casserole. Dry the pheasant with kitchen paper, add to the casserole and fry until lightly browned on all sides. Season with salt and pepper, spoon over the marmalade, add the thyme and a slug of the wine, cover and cook in the oven for 30–40 minutes. Remove the pheasant from the casserole and set aside in a warm place, covered, to rest. Keep the casserole, with the fat inside, to one side.

While the pheasant is cooking, put the milk for the bread sauce into a pan with the halved onion, cloves, bay leaf and peppercorns.

Bring just to the boil, then remove from the heat and leave to infuse for 20 minutes or so. Strain the milk back into the pan and add the breadcrumbs, some seasoning and the butter. Simmer gently for a couple of minutes, then cover and keep warm. If it looks too stodgy when you come to serve the pheasant, add a spoonful of cream.

Place the casserole with the fat from the pheasant over a medium heat, add the flour and cook, then add the rest of the wine and cook down, adding some cooking water from any vegetables you're cooking. Stir until smooth and pour into a warmed jug. Serve the pheasant with the gravy and bread sauce.

# BEEF STEW WITH DUMPLINGS

Serves 4

2 tbsp olive or rapeseed oil
600g blade steak, trimmed and cut into chunks
30g butter
1 onion, sliced
30g plain flour
Dash of red wine
500ml meat stock (cubes are fine)
3 carrots, chopped
Good pinch of herbes de Provence
1–1½ tsp chilli paste or flakes
3 tbsp marmalade
Salt and freshly ground black pepper

**For the dumplings**
115g self-raising flour
65g cold unsalted butter

Heat the oil until smoking in a large flameproof casserole, add the meat and brown quickly on all sides. Remove to a plate.

Melt the butter in the casserole, add the onion and fry until soft. Stir in the flour and cook to make a roux. Add the wine and slowly add the stock, stirring well until it comes to the boil. Return the meat to the pan and add the carrots, herbs, chilli, marmalade and some seasoning. Cover the casserole with baking parchment and then add the lid, and cook slowly for 2

hours, either over a low heat on the hob or in the oven at 150°C/130°C fan/Gas 2.

To make the dumplings, sift the flour into a bowl, grate in the butter, add some seasoning and mix well with your hands until a dough is formed. Divide into about 12 balls and roll into dumplings. 30 minutes before the end of the cooking time, place them on top of the stew and put the lid back on. They will absorb plenty of liquid, so

## CHILDHOOD MEMORIES

We lived in our father's parliamentary constituency, and there were endless local meetings and parties. One evening when there was a cheese and wine party at home, one of the kind Conservative ladies decided that we children needed feeding and cooked us a fine stew for supper. It was only the next day when my mother couldn't find the dog food that she discovered we had eaten it; we thought it was odd that the lady had failed to notice the warning green dye on the meat.

# BITTER ORANGE AND CARDAMOM COCKTAIL

Serves 6

12 cardamom pods
6 tbsp Seville orange marmalade,
  plus extra to serve
400ml vodka
125ml Cointreau
4 tbsp lemon juice
Ice, to serve

Bash 6 of the cardamom pods in a pestle and mortar until they split.

Melt the marmalade in a pan, then whisk in the vodka. Add the crushed cardamom pods. Warm the mix, but don't let it boil. Leave to infuse off the heat for 20 minutes, then strain.

Add the Cointreau and lemon juice and chill (or keep in the freezer). Serve in glasses with a little more marmalade in the bottom, ice and a cardamom pod floating on top.

# VEGAN ORANGE COOKIES

Makes about 20

110g dairy-free butter, at room temperature

115g golden granulated sugar

2 tsp orange extract

250g plain flour

1 tsp bicarbonate of soda

Pinch of salt

Grated zest of 1 sweet orange

2 tbsp dairy-free milk

2 tbsp candied Seville orange peel (see page 68), chopped

**For the glaze**

120g icing sugar

Juice of 1 orange (use the zested one)

½ tsp orange extract

A few drops of orange food colouring

Heat the oven to 180°C/160°C fan/Gas 4.

Line a baking tray with baking parchment.

Cream the butter and sugar together in the bowl of a food mixer. Add in the orange extract.

Stir in the flour, bicarb and salt until well mixed, then add the orange zest. Stir in the milk and candied peel and combine thoroughly.

Separate the dough into about 20 pieces, roll each in your hands to form a ball and place them slightly apart on a baking tray. Flatten each slightly using a fork dipped in cold water.

Bake for about 12 minutes, until just browned on top. Remove and leave to cool.

Combine the glaze ingredients in a small bowl and spoon over the cookies once they are completely cold.

SPRING

If you're ever in Seville around Easter, when bitter orange trees are flowering, the warm Sevillian air mixed with the heady scent of orange can be intoxicating. There's nothing quite like it. While it's a traditional winter pastime, marmalade can be made all year round; you simply have to be organised and plan ahead. Whole oranges freeze beautifully, so now's the time to take them out of the freezer and start simmering.

MARCH

# MARMALADE WHISKY SOUR COCKTAIL

Serves 1

Ice
70ml bourbon
30ml lemon juice
20ml sugar syrup
1 tsp orange marmalade
1 dash of orange bitters
1 slice of orange peel

Fill a cocktail shaker with ice. Add all the remaining ingredients except the orange twist and shake vigorously for 30 seconds to dissolve the marmalade.

Strain into a chilled martini glass and garnish with the orange peel.

# PINK GRAPEFRUIT MARMALADE

This is a bright, fresh marmalade with a beautiful colour.

Makes about 5 x 450g jars

**2 pink or red grapefruit**
**4 Seville oranges, defrosted if frozen**
**About 1kg granulated or preserving sugar**
**2 lemons**

Have a large preserving pan ready and a bowl lined with muslin.

Wash and weigh the grapefruit and oranges, and make a note of the total weight. Cut all of them in half, squeeze the orange juice and add to the pan, adding the membranes and pips to the muslin. Chop the grapefruit halves into pieces and cut the orange peels as small or finely as you like – I like largeish matchsticks. (Some grapefruit pith is very thick and you will need to cut it off and add to the muslin cloth with the pips and any other odds and ends of peel.)

Multiply the original weight of the fruit by 2.25 and pour the same weight of cold water into the pan. Add the chopped fruit, knot the muslin cloth, submerge it in the fruit, and leave to soak overnight.

The next day, bring to the boil and simmer for about 2 hours until soft. Remove from the heat and leave to soak overnight again, if possible.

Measure the pulp and add sugar to a ratio of 4:3 fruit to sugar. Juice the lemons and add the juice to the pan. Heat slowly until the sugar is entirely dissolved, then turn up to full heat and boil fast until the mixture reads 105°C on a sugar thermometer (or use a cold saucer to test for setting point, see page 9). Halfway through cooking, turn the oven to 150°C/130°C fan/Gas 2, and see page 9 to sterilise and seal the jars.

When the marmalade is at 105°C or shows signs of wrinkling on a cold saucer, remove the pan from the heat and allow to settle for 20 minutes.

Fill the warm jars to the top and place the lids on (see page 9). Wipe and label when cool.

# CANDIED SEVILLE ORANGE PEEL

You can also use sweet oranges in place of Seville for these. Coat them in chocolate as shown here, and give them away as presents, or chop them and put them in the buttercream filling for macarons (see page 177), on cakes and in cookies.

Makes 15–20

**2 Seville oranges**
**200g granulated or preserving sugar**
**250ml cold water**
**About 150g dark chocolate**
  **(70% cocoa solids),**
  **broken into pieces (optional)**

Cut the oranges in half and juice them. Cut each half into two, carefully slice off the thick pith from the inside (you can leave some of it on) and cut the peel into strips 5mm–1cm wide.

Add them to a pan of boiling water, bring back to the boil and simmer for 5 minutes. Drain, rinse with cold water and repeat this twice more with fresh boiling water.

Put the sugar and 250ml cold water in a pan and set over a low heat to dissolve the sugar (don't let it boil). Add the drained slices of peel and let them cook gently until the syrup has almost all gone.

Place the peel strips on a cooling rack set over baking parchment and leave to dry. They will take around 24 hours. When they're no longer sticky, either coat in chocolate (as below) or store them in a plastic container with a lid.

To coat in chocolate, melt the chocolate in a heatproof bowl suspended over a pan of simmering water, making sure the base of the bowl isn't touching the water. Dip the strips of peel into the melted chocolate – either dip just one end, or use two forks and coat them entirely in chocolate. Lay them on baking parchment to dry and put in the fridge for 30 minutes to harden.

# CUSTARD TARTS WITH CANDIED SEVILLE ORANGES

Makes 12

1 large egg, plus 2 yolks
115g caster sugar
2 tbsp cornflour
400ml milk
1 tsp vanilla extract
1 x 350g sheet of puff pastry
Freshly grated nutmeg
12 small pieces of candied
  Seville orange peel (see page 68)

Grease a 12-hole muffin tin and heat the oven to 200°C/180°C fan/Gas 6.

Off the heat, use a balloon whisk to mix the egg, egg yolks, sugar and cornflour in a pan, then slowly whisk in the milk until well mixed.

Place the pan over medium heat and, using a wooden spoon, stir until the custard thickens up and comes to the boil. Take off the heat and add the vanilla, then pour into a bowl and cover with cling film to cool.

Roll out the pastry so you have a rectangle of about 30 x 40cm, and about 2mm thick. Brush with a small amount of water, sprinkle with grated nutmeg and, starting on a long side, roll up the pastry tightly to make a log. Cut in half and then slice each half into 6 round pieces. Place the pastry wheels flat on a lightly floured work surface and flatten them slightly with your fingers or a rolling pin, then put each disc into a hole of the muffin tin and ease the pastry carefully up the sides until just above the rim. (Wetting your thumb with water makes this easier.)

Part-bake in the oven for 8 minutes then remove from the oven. Push the pastry up the sides using the back of a teaspoon, to make space for the custard.

Spoon in the custard and cook in the oven for 10 minutes until the custard is soft but a little scorched on top. Let them cool in the muffin tin for 5–10 minutes, then add a small piece of candied orange to the top of each.

Citrus fruits are very grand and can trace their family tree back perhaps some eight million years. A few years ago, scientists discovered in the western Yunnan province of China a fossilised citrus leaf from Citrus linczangensis, an ancient ancestor of the sixty or so citrus species now found worldwide. It had begun from just three – Citrus medica, Citrus maxima and Citrus reticulata: citron, pomelo, mandarin – in the Himalayan foothills.

Bitter oranges reached Arabia in the 9th century, Sicily in the 11th and southern Spain at the end of the 12th. Sour oranges were arriving at London and Bristol docks at the end of the 15th century: pips were planted by the Carew family at Beddington in Surrey, from oranges brought to England by Sir Walter Raleigh, and were bearing fruit by 1595, but a hard winter in 1739 killed them off. But bitter orange trees are tough little chaps and not pampered princesses: they have good strong roots, flourish in tropical climates but can put up with some frost; they readily self-seed and in Spain there are trees rumoured to be 600 years old. One treasured tree in a tub at Versailles was apparently planted in 1421, unlikely but possibly, to celebrate the birth of Henry VI of England, later the disputed King of France.

In Britain we mostly use sour oranges for marmalade, but there is so much more to them than that. The tree's fine-grained pale wood is valued for inlays and cabinet making, and the fruit has been used for wine and liqueurs, as soap and as a wood cleaner, and as a stomach remedy. Petitgrain oil, distilled from immature oranges and leaves, boosts the immune system and, like lavender and bergamot, is known for its relaxing qualities. The juice of bitter oranges is antiseptic and used in fitness products. The flowers are made into neroli oil both for the perfume industry and as a sedative, the leaves as a stimulant and for stomach disorders, the bark for fevers and as an anti-parasitic. Burning dried peel keeps mosquitoes and ants away, bees surge to orange trees in blossom for outstanding honey – the list is endless. Citrus aurantium, like Mary Poppins, can turn its hand to just about anything.

# CHICKEN WITH SEVILLE ORANGES

Serves 6

1 lemon, halved
25g butter
1 large free-range chicken
2 Seville oranges
100ml olive oil
2 shallots, chopped
1 garlic clove, chopped
A few leaves of thyme and rosemary
2 tsp Dijon mustard
3 chicory bulbs, halved
Salt and freshly ground black pepper

Put one lemon half and the butter inside the chicken's cavity and squeeze the juice from the second lemon half and set aside. Heat the oven to 190°C/170°C fan/Gas 5.

Grate the zest from the two oranges into the bowl of a food processor, then peel them and add the orange segments (removing the pips) to the processor. Add the olive oil, shallots, garlic, herbs, mustard, the reserved lemon juice and some salt and pepper, and whizz to combine.

continued overleaf

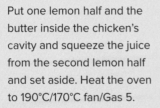

Using your hands, spread the mixture over the chicken and place it breast side down in a roasting tin. Add a cup of water to the bottom of the tin and roast for 30 minutes, then turn the chicken breast-side up and arrange the chicory halves round it. Baste and roast for another 30–40 minutes, depending on its size. Pull back a leg I to check it's not too pink and that the juices are running clear.

Remove the chicken and chicory and allow the chicken to rest for 10 minutes while you make gravy with the pan juices.

APRIL

# BERTIE'S FOUR-FRUIT MARMALADE

**M**y friend Bertie's recipe is from his aunt Jane Simpson, who sixty years ago had Seville orange trees planted in her vegetable garden on their farm Sewefontein in Citrusdal, South Africa, to make enough marmalade for Bertie's Uncle Peter and their many friends. Bertie continues the tradition of making quite a lot of the same marmalade each year for himself and his friends.

Makes about 8–10 x 450g jars

1 pink grapefruit
2 lemons
4 limes
8 Seville oranges, defrosted if frozen
2 litres water
1.5kg granulated sugar

Halve all the fruit and squeeze the juice into a jug, keeping the pips in a muslin bag.

Remove as much pith as possible from 6 of the squeezed-out Sevilles and 2 of the limes, adding the pith to the muslin bag.

continued overleaf

Put the remaining squeezed-out skins in a preserving pan and cover with the water. Tie up the muslin bag and put it in the pan.

Slice the pith-free 6 Sevilles and 2 limes as thinly as possible into shreds, and add these to the jug of juice. Leave these and the contents of the pan to soak overnight.

The next day, bring the contents of the preserving pan to the boil and let simmer for 1–2 hours, until soft and you can easily squash the peel with a wooden spoon. Remove from the heat and leave to soak overnight.

The following day, heat the oven to 180°C/160°C fan/Gas 4 and put the sugar in a heatproof bowl for 15 minutes to warm up.

Place the preserving pan over a low heat and remove all the skins, squeezing them as you remove them to get as much of the juices as possible out of them. Remove the muslin bag, and squeeze out the juice. Turn the oven down to 150°C/130°C fan/Gas 2 and place the jars in to warm up and sterilise, adding the lids for the last 5 minutes. (see page 9)

Add the jug of juice and shreds of skin to the pan, then the warmed sugar. Stir until fully dissolved, then bring to the boil. Boil for 1 hour, measuring the temperature as you go until it reaches 104.2°C (or test for setting point using the wrinkle test, see page 9).

Take the pan off the heat and remove as much of the scum as possible from the surface (generally not much). Leave to settle for at least 15–20 minutes before transferring to the warm jars, sealing with lids and labelling once cool (see page 9). It will keep in a dark cupboard for at least a year.

# MARMALADE VODKA

Makes 1 litre

**4–5 tbsp dark, bitter marmalade
(see page 47 for homemade)**
**1 litre vodka**

Put the marmalade in a large lidded or preserving glass jar. Pour over the vodka and leave for 2 weeks, shaking occasionally.

Strain and pour into bottles.

# FLORENTINES

Makes 18

Vegetable oil, for greasing
45g butter
60g demerara sugar
60g candied Seville orange peel
 (see page 68), chopped
30g dried cranberries
20g shelled pistachios, roughly chopped
60g blanched almonds, cut into slivers
15g plain flour
Pinch of salt
1 tbsp double cream
200g dark chocolate (70% cocoa solids),
 broken into pieces

Heat the oven to 180°C/160°C fan/Gas 4 and line two baking trays with baking parchment brushed with vegetable oil.

Melt the butter and sugar together in a pan over medium heat. Put the fruit and nuts in a bowl, sift over the flour and mix well.

Remove the pan from the heat and stir in the salt and cream, then the fruit and nuts. Drop teaspoons of the mixture onto the baking trays and, using a fork dipped in water, gently flatten them out thinly (without making holes), leaving space for them to spread as they cook.

Bake for about 10–12 minutes until golden brown all over, then leave to cool on the trays.

When cool, melt half the chocolate in a heatproof bowl set over a pan of simmering water, making sure the base of the bowl doesn't touch the water. Stir occasionally until fully melted.

Carefully dip the underside of each florentine in the chocolate and leave to cool and set.

If you prefer a smoother finish, you can dip them again for a second coat once they have set, melting the chocolate again to do so. Do those wavy fork lines if you want. Let them harden before serving or storing in an airtight box.

# PORK CHOPS WITH MARMALADE, FENNEL AND ROSEMARY

Serves 2

2 pork chops (bone-in gives more flavour)
Juice of 1 Seville orange
Salt and freshly ground black pepper

**For the marinade**
2 tbsp olive oil
A few sprigs of rosemary
2 tbsp marmalade
½ onion, chopped
Small piece of fresh ginger, sliced and peeled
½ fennel bulb, sliced

Put the chops and marinade ingredients into a plastic food bag and mix well. Marinate on a plate in the fridge for at least 30 minutes, longer if possible.

Heat a frying pan over medium-high heat and tip in the contents of the bag. Cook the chops for about 4 minutes on each side, until cooked right through, then remove and keep warm on a plate.

Add the Seville orange juice to the pan and boil to reduce the sauce. Strain the marinade, return to the pan, add back the chops and heat through.

Serve with baked potatoes and green veg or cauliflower cheese.

The Moors – North African nomadic Muslims who settled in Spain, Sicily and part of France for 700 years in the Middle Ages – discovered bitter orange trees in Asia and brought them to Europe in the 11th century. The flowers and leaves had long been used in Chinese medicine as diuretics, for chest congestion, cleansing the blood and regulating the qi. By the late 1400s bitter oranges were arriving in English ports: it was believed they had aphrodisiac qualities, heating the blood, and Mary Tudor hoped that eating marmalade (or the version of it made with quince, as described on page 44) would help her conceive a son – it didn't.

When sweet Chinese oranges reached Britain, Restoration prostitutes found selling oranges to be an excellent marketing device. Orange Girls thronged around the theatres and Eleanor Gwyn (Samuel Pepys's 'pretty, witty Nell') made swift progress from orange seller to the stage, became a popular comedy turn, and from there it was a mere hop to the king's bed.

The 17th century doctor William Salmon advised lemon and citron peels for the stomach, for headaches and those all-important melancholic humours.

These days bitter orange extract is used for heartburn and insomnia. Some weight loss and bodybuilding supplements contain bitter orange extract which, combined with caffeine, acts as a mild stimulant and can cause high blood pressure and increased heart rate, so needs to be taken with care and under advice. Topically, it's anti-fungal and antiseptic and works wonders on problem skin, athlete's foot and, er, jock itch.

# MY AUNT MARGARET'S SHORTBREAD

**M**argaret lived at Goodnestone in East Kent, and visitors flocked to see her garden – and especially her tearooms. She had an ancient Aga which churned out endless cakes, scones and flapjacks. Her shortbread was outstanding and she would have told me off for adding marmalade peel to it.

Makes 16 pieces

210g butter
85g caster sugar
255g plain flour
85g cornflour or semolina
Pinch of salt
35g marmalade peel
  (from a jar of marmalade)
½ tsp orange or vanilla extract

Heat the oven to 180°C/160°C fan/Gas 4 and line a 24cm square baking tin with baking parchment.

Beat the butter and sugar together in an electric mixer, then add the flours and salt. Mix thoroughly, add the orange peel and extract, mix quickly and turn the mixture into the tin. Press down firmly with your fingers and spread the top smooth with a knife.

Bake for 25 minutes until lightly browned, then move to a lower shelf of the oven, turn the temperature down to 140°C/120°C fan/Gas 1 and bake for about another hour, checking occasionally, to avoid a soggy middle. Leave to cool in the tin for 10 minutes, but lightly score the pieces out. Turn onto a wire rack to cool completely, before separating into pieces.

MAY

# GINGER MARMALADE

It may look like a lot of fresh ginger to chop, but do chop it by hand or with a herb chopper – I have tried putting it in the food processor and it seems to bruise the ginger and affect the flavour. Should you want to make more or less of this, my sugar ratio is 3:4 sugar to pulp. My ratio of water to chopped fruit is about 2.3:1, so for 1 kilo of fruit I add about 2.3 litres of water.

Makes 5–6 x 450g jars

**1kg Seville oranges, defrosted if frozen**
**250g lemons (2–3 lemons), plus the juice of 2 extra**
**2.8 litres water**
**About 1.4kg granulated or preserving sugar**
**About 1 tsp ground ginger**
**About 110g fresh ginger, peeled and chopped**

Scrub the oranges and lemons and remove the stalks. Have ready a bowl lined with a clean muslin cloth for the pips and membranes, and excess pith, and a preserving pan.

Quarter the lemons, halve and juice the oranges, and slice the peels into slightly-bigger-than-matchstick size. If the white pith is very thick, shave some of it away from the inside of the peel and put it in the muslin with the pips, but don't cut it all away.

continued overleaf

Add the water, knot the muslin cloth and push it under the fruit and water. Leave to soak overnight.

The next day, bring the fruit and water to the boil and allow it to simmer gently for about 2 hours, pushing the bag under the water occasionally, until you can easily squash the peel with a wooden spoon. Remove from the heat, cover and ideally leave it for another 24 hours.

Remove the muslin bag and place it in a sieve over a bowl to drain, squashing it gently to remove as much liquid as possible. Measure the volume of pulp and add the sugar in a ratio of 3:4 sugar to pulp, and the juice of the 2 lemons. For each litre of pulp, add ½ tsp ground ginger and 60g chopped fresh ginger.

Stir over a low heat until the sugar is completely melted and you have a smooth, warm syrup. Turn the heat up high under the pan. When the mixture reaches 102°C, switch on your oven to 150°C/130°C fan/Gas 2 and warm the jars, right way up, and then lids for the last 5 minutes (see page 9). Once the marmalade is boiling, it will take 30 minutes or more to reach a set.

Stir the marmalade occasionally, watching the way the drips fall off the spoon, and when the drops join together and hang like icicles, you are nearly there. Once the temperature reaches 105°C (or setting point when using the wrinkle test, see page 9), take the pan from the heat and let it cool and settle for 15–20 minutes, before transferring to the warm jars using the sterilising and sealing methods (see page 9) and leave in a cool place, undisturbed, until cold.

# MARMALADE FRENCH TOAST

A very slightly indulgent
breakfast sandwich

Serves 1

**2 slices of white sourdough bread**
**1 heaped tbsp marmalade**
**2 eggs**
**1 tbsp double cream**
**Tiny pinch of dried rosemary**
**1 tsp sugar**
**Knob of butter**

Spread one of the bread
slices with the marmalade
and sandwich together.

In a shallow bowl, whisk
together the eggs, cream,
dried rosemary and sugar.
Dip the sandwich in the
mixture, soak well and turn
over.

Melt the butter in a frying
pan until sizzling and cook
the sandwich for a couple of
minutes each side. Cut in half
to serve.

**M**rs Beeton offers several recipes for marmalade in her *Book of Household Management*. She estimates that a batch of homemade marmalade would take three hours at a cost of 6d per jar (£1.60 today). But even she, practical and youthful as she was (she died woefully young, at the age of twenty-eight), could not help adding: 'The best marmalade is made by Keiller, and many are of the opinion that when it can be bought so cheaply and good it is scarcely worth making it at home.' At that time James Keiller & Son were making their famous marmalade in a Guernsey factory to avoid the 1846 sugar tax.

I always imagined Mrs Beeton as a stout old lady, something like Queen Victoria with a rolling pin, but I was wrong. She grew up as one of the eldest in a family of seventeen children, which must have given her some early insights into the challenges of household management. She finished her education in Heidelberg; she was a journalist, a gifted piano player and pastry maker, and she began collecting the recipes for her famous book aged twenty-two — it sold a massive 60,000 copies in 1861, the year of publication. No household of the day was complete without a copy.

# SCALLOPS WITH SPINACH AND SEVILLE ORANGES

Serves 4

**500g frozen scallops**
**250g brown or white rice**
**30g butter**
**Small bag of spinach, washed**
**Juice of 2 Seville oranges**
**Salt and freshly ground black pepper**

Allow about 30 minutes to defrost the scallops, pat them dry with kitchen paper and sprinkle with salt and pepper.

Cook the rice according to the packet instructions, or your usual way.

Just before the rice is cooked, melt the butter in a frying pan over medium heat and cook the scallops for about 2½ minutes each side, then remove them to a dish.

Add the spinach to the frying pan, stirring while it cooks down. Add the orange juice, heat through thoroughly, replace the scallops for a moment and serve with the cooked rice.

# CANTUCCINI WITH ORANGE AND PISTACHIO

Makes about 30

4 tbsp olive oil
150g caster sugar
2 tsp vanilla extract
1 tsp orange extract
2 eggs, beaten
225g plain flour
1 tsp baking powder
Pinch of salt
125g shelled pistachios, chopped
75g candied Seville orange peel
  (see page 68), chopped

Heat the oven to 160°C/140°C fan/Gas 3. Line a baking tray with parchment.

Mix the oil and sugar in a large bowl until well blended. Add the vanilla and orange extracts, then beat in the eggs. Sift the flour into another bowl, add the baking powder and salt and gradually stir into the egg mixture. Fold in the pistachios and candied orange peel.

Divide the dough in half; run your hands under a cold tap to make handling the dough easier. Form two rolls about 30cm long and 5cm wide and place them on the baking tray. Leave plenty of space between the logs as they will spread out.

Bake for about 30 minutes until light brown. Remove from the oven and set aside to cool for 10 minutes, turning the oven down to 140°C/120°C fan/Gas 1.

Using a sharp serrated knife, cut the logs on the diagonal into 1cm-thick slices. Lie them flat on their cut sides on the lined tray and bake for another 15–20 minutes, or until crisp and dry. Cool on wire rack.

SUMMER

Open the windows and fill the house with the smell of citrus. Summer is the perfect time to try some sharp new marmalade, with limes or lemons. Look around your garden for herbs – thyme, rosemary or lavender for a fresh botanical flavour. Lemons are always a great alternative and available all year round to try something slightly different, so why not make a few jars of lemon marmalade for an unusual taste and a welcome present.

JUNE

# ALLY'S MARMALADE ICE CREAM

**T**his ice cream recipe is from my friend, Ally Bolitho, who lives near Penzance in the very farthest tip of Cornwall. This doesn't need churning, and stays semi-freddo, so it can be served straight from the freezer.

Makes about 900ml/Serves 8

500ml double cream
1 x 397g tin condensed milk
Grated zest of 2 oranges
2 tbsp Cointreau
1 smallish jar of dark marmalade, (200-250g)
  chopped up in a food processor

Whip the cream to firm peaks but do not over-whip, then add the condensed milk very gradually, mixing well, followed by the zest, Cointreau and chopped marmalade.

Spoon or pour into a suitable container and freeze.

## CHILDHOOD MEMORIES

Ice cream was the most tremendous treat when we were young. There might very occasionally be a block of vanilla ice cream, cut into slices and served with whichever stewed fruit was open that day – blackcurrants, or rhubarb, or there was the anticipation of the ice-cream van. After lunch on Sunday we would listen out for the jingle of its bells and dash down to the end of the drive, where we waited patiently for what seemed like the whole afternoon. Sometimes the van went a different way and never came past at all. My mother remarked that with five children it was the most peaceful afternoon of the week.

# LIME
# MARMALADE

I think lime marmalade needs delicate slivers of peel, so cut the fruit for this marmalade into the finest slices you can manage without cutting yourself.

Makes 5–6 x 450g jars

**500g limes (4–6 limes)**
**350g Seville oranges (about 3),**
  **defrosted if frozen**
**About 2 litres water**
**About 1.3kg granulated**
  **or preserving sugar**
**Juice of 2 lemons**

Scrub and weigh the limes and oranges.

Cut the fruit into fine slices, putting all pips, ends of fruit and excess orange pith into a muslin bag. Put the slices in a preserving pan and add the water (2.3 times the weight of whole fruit) and muslin bag. Leave to soak overnight.

The next day, simmer for 2 hours until tender – lime peel is tough so make sure that you can easily cut it with a wooden spoon. Cover and leave overnight.

The next day, remove the muslin bag, squeezing the juice out into the pan, and measure the volume of pulp. Add sugar to the ratio of 3:4 sugar:fruit and add the lemon juice. Stir over a low heat until the sugar is entirely dissolved.

Bring to a fast boil, and use the sterilising method (see page 9). Check the temperature from time to time and when the marmalade reaches 105°C (or check the setting point using the wrinkle test on page 9), remove from the heat and leave to stand for 15–20 minutes. Meanwhile, put the lids in the oven for 5 minutes to sterilise (see page 9).

Pot into warm jars and seal (see page 9) and leave undisturbed until cool.

**W**e think of marmalade as peculiarly British, but at the Dalemain Festival in Cumbria the Japanese are among the most enthusiastic competitors, producing exquisitely packaged jars, and now hold their own competition at Yawatahama. It seems there is a real feel for marmalade-making in Japan, and not just because there are some forty citrus varieties available, mostly growing on Shikoku Island in the south. In the book *Ikigai: The Japanese Secret to a Long and Happy Life*, the authors explore the way the Japanese people find joy and purpose in work and community; making marmalade must also chime with their concept of mottainai (not wasting a thing).

Australia, too, now has an annual marmalade festival in Beaumont House in Adelaide ('Dalemain Down Under') and previous winners included mandarin marmalade, cumquat and tangelo marmalade, cumquat liqueur grapefruit marmalade, tangelo and limoncello marmalade and tangelo and Cointreau marmalade. Gin also featured. It's astonishing that from three basic ingredients – citrus, water, sugar – not a single recipe for homemade marmalade will look or taste the same. Making marmalade requires a bit of patience and focus; it's immersive and the end result is super-satisfying. No wonder we all get so jolly competitive.

# WARM DUCK SALAD

Serves 4 as a main course, or 8 for a first course or lunch

4 medium potatoes, peeled
2 uncooked beetroot
1 fennel bulb, finely sliced
Couple of sprigs of rosemary
4 tbsp olive oil, plus extra for rubbing on the duck
4 duck breasts
Bag of watercress, thick stalks removed
1 heaped tbsp marmalade
Grated zest and juice of 1 Seville or sweet orange
A few slices of fresh ginger, peeled
Handful of walnut halves or pieces
Salt and freshly ground black pepper

Combine the dressing ingredients in a jar and shake well. Heat the oven to 200°C/180°C fan/Gas 6.

Parboil the potatoes and beetroot in separate pans for 12 minutes, then, wearing rubber gloves, run the beetroot under a cold tap and remove the skins. Dice them and the potatoes into 2cm squares and add to a roasting tin with the fennel, rosemary and oil. Mix well and roast in the oven for about 40 minutes until the potatoes are crisp and brown.

When the vegetables have been in the oven for 20 minutes, lightly score a diamond pattern into the skin of the duck breasts and rub with oil and salt. Place them skin-side down in a cold frying pan over medium heat and cook slowly for about 10 minutes, so that the fat renders down and the skin crisps. Turn them over and cook the other side for 30 seconds to seal. Remove them to a roasting dish, skin-side down, and finish them in the hot oven for 6–8 minutes.

Remove the duck from the oven and set aside to rest.

Stir the marmalade, orange zest and juice, ginger and some salt and pepper into the duck juices in the frying pan and cook until bubbling, then add the walnuts. Slice the duck breasts and arrange on top of the vegetables. Spoon over the warm frying-pan glaze and walnuts, and serve.

JULY

# SALMON WITH MARMALADE GLAZE

These salmon fillets would be good served on a pile of green leaves with red and yellow peppers that have been grilled until the skins have blackened, peeled and cut into strips.

Serves 4

**4 salmon fillets**

**For the glaze**
**2 tbsp Seville orange marmalade**
**2 tbsp light soy sauce**
**1 tsp paprika**
**Thumb-sized piece of fresh ginger, peeled and grated**
**1 tbsp olive oil**
**Salt and freshly ground black pepper**

Heat the oven to 210°C/190°C fan/Gas 7. On a lightly greased baking tray, lay the salmon fillets skin-side down.

Mix together all the glaze ingredients, with salt and pepper to taste, and spoon it evenly over the fish.

Bake in the oven for 10–12 minutes or until the salmon is still pink inside.

# LEMON AND EARL GREY MARMALADE

Bergamot oranges have a lovely scent and are in season when Seville oranges are, January–February. If you want a paler marmalade, leave out the tea and add a total of 1.75ml of cold water instead.

Makes about 6 x 450g jars

**4 Earl Grey tea bags**
**500ml boiling water**
**500g lemons (4–5 lemons), plus the juice of 1 lemon**
**2 bergamot oranges (about 400g)**
**1.25 litres cold water**
**About 1kg granulated or preserving sugar**

Put the tea bags into a heatproof jug or bowl, pour over the boiling water and leave to infuse and cool slightly.

Weigh and scrub the fruit, noting down the weight, remove the stalks and cut into quarters. Slice them finely, adding the pips to a muslin-lined bowl. Add the sliced fruit to a preserving pan with the cold water and strained tea. Knot the muslin and push it under the fruit and water. If possible, leave to soak overnight.

Bring the fruit to the boil and allow it to simmer gently for about 1½ hours, pushing the muslin bag under the liquid occasionally, until you can easily squash the peel with a wooden spoon. Remove from the heat, cover and ideally leave it overnight again, or for a couple of hours.

Remove the muslin bag and place it in a sieve over a bowl to drain, squashing it gently to remove as much liquid as possible. Measure the volume of pulp and add sugar to a ratio of 4:3, so to each 100ml of pulp, add 75g sugar. Add the lemon juice and squeezed- out juice from the muslin bag to the pan.

Stir over a low heat until every grain of sugar has melted and you have a smooth, warm syrup. Turn the heat up high under the pan and switch on your oven to 150°C/130° fan/ Gas 2. Once the marmalade is boiling it will take at least 20 minutes to reach a set. Put the baking tray of jars, right way up, in the oven for 15 minutes.

Stir the marmalade occasionally, and once the temperature reaches 105°C (or test using the wrinkle test on page 9), take the pan from the heat and let it cool and settle for 15 minutes. Use the sterilising and sealing methods to transfer the marmalade (see page 9).

# MARMALADE COOKIES

This recipe is adapted from my good friend Troels Bendix, Danish super-baker and founder of SØDT Bakery.

Makes 20–24

**155g unsalted butter, softened**

**65g caster sugar**

**90g soft brown sugar**

**1 egg, plus 1 yolk**

**140g plain flour**

**175g oats**

**2 scant tsp bicarbonate of soda**

**Pinch of salt**

**1 tsp ground ginger**

**Pinch of freshly grated nutmeg**

**2 tbsp marmalade, mostly rind, chopped**

**1 tsp grated orange zest**

**1 tsp orange extract**

Heat the oven to 180°C/160°C fan/Gas 4 and line 2 or 3 baking trays with baking parchment (or cook them in batches on one tray).

Cream the butter and both sugars in an electric stand mixer until soft and pale. Add the egg and yolk, and mix. Add the flour, oats, bicarb, salt and spices and mix, taking care not to overmix, then stir in the marmalade, orange zest and extract.

Divide the mixture into 20–24 pieces, about 35g each, and roll each into a ball using your hands. Space them well apart on the lined baking trays and bake for about 12 minutes.

Allow to cool for a few minutes then slide off and put on to a wire rack to cool. They should be slightly soft and chewy.

**M**armalade has often provided a piece of home for travellers. The officers' families brought marmalade with them to India during the years of British rule, and eventually took to making their own from the pomelo, a large grapefruit-like citrus fruit. Captain Scott took a jar to Antarctica in 1910 and the jar was found years later, poignantly buried in the ice and probably still edible. Paddington Bear carried marmalade sandwiches in his hat for emergencies and Edmund Hillary thought it worthwhile to carry a jar up Mount Everest. Red Cross parcels sent to serving soldiers during the Second World War often contained a tin of marmalade. Sometimes nothing else will do.

# CHICKEN WITH MARMALADE

Serves 4

8–10 free-range chicken pieces
  (thighs, drumsticks, half-breasts)
1 tsp cumin seeds
1 tbsp olive oil
½ a glass of white wine
5 tbsp dark marmalade

Heat the oven to 200°C/180°C fan/Gas 6. Place the chicken pieces in an ovenproof dish.

Heat a small frying pan until hot, add the cumin seeds and toast for a couple of minutes, until fragrant.

Combine the oil, wine, marmalade and toasted cumin seeds in a small bowl, stir well and spoon over the chicken.

Bake for 18–20 minutes, until cooked through, basting once or twice, and serve with something like sautéed potatoes and fresh green vegetables or red cabbage.

# HOT MARMALADE SOUFFLÉS

**I** must have been mad, but many years ago when my children were tiny I regularly made these for dinner parties, apologising to everyone for the roar of the electric whisk when I put the last-minute egg whites in. They are unbelievably fragrant when you put the spoon into them. I often make small ones in advance and freeze them (as soon as you have spooned the mixture into the dishes). On the day, cook the small ones straight from the freezer for 12–15 minutes so that the centres are heated right through but still soft.

Serves 4

4 large eggs, separated
125g caster sugar
50g plain flour, sifted
250ml milk
4 tbsp Grand Marnier
2 tbsp fine-cut orange marmalade
Grated zest of 1 orange
Icing sugar, for dusting

You will need a 1.25-litre soufflé dish or 4 individual 250ml soufflé dishes, buttered and sugared.

In a heatproof bowl, whisk the egg yolks with half the sugar until pale and thick. Fold in the flour.

Bring the milk to the boil in a pan and pour it over the egg and sugar mixture, stirring well, then return the mixture to the pan and cook over a low heat, stirring with a wooden spoon. When you have a smooth, thick custard, take the pan from the heat and stir in the Grand Marnier, marmalade and orange zest. Cover with cling film and leave to cool for 30 minutes.

Heat the oven to 220°C/200°C fan/Gas 7.

Whisk the egg whites until soft peaks form, then gradually whisk in the remaining sugar. Add a spoonful of the whisked whites to the cooled custard and stir it in, then fold in the rest of the whites and spoon the mixture evenly into your prepared soufflé dish/es.

Cook the large soufflé for 15–20 minutes or the small ones for about 9 minutes, until risen and browned but still wobbly. Serve immediately with cream.

AUGUST

# BITTER ORANGE MARINADE (FOR CHICKEN AND PORK)

Makes about 300ml
(enough for a dish to serve 8)

**3 Seville oranges**
**5 garlic cloves, chopped**
**3 tbsp olive oil**
**Small handful of fresh oregano, chopped**
**1 bay leaf, chopped**
**Pinch of ground cumin**
**1 tsp chilli paste or 1 fresh chilli,**
   **deseeded and chopped**

Halve the bitter oranges and juice them. Add the remaining ingredients to the juice and combine well.

Put chicken or pork pieces in a sealable plastic food bag, add the marinade and leave to marinate for at least an hour, or overnight, in the fridge.

Once the meat is removed for cooking, throw the marinade away.

# LAVENDER MARMALADE

**I**f you have some Seville oranges in your freezer, then try making this lavender marmalade in July/ August when the lavender is out. As always, it's good to leave the fruit infusing overnight before and after cooking. You could also make this with tiny thyme leaves and flowers instead of the lavender, adding sprigs to the muslin bag and some flowers or tiny leaves just before potting up.

Makes 4–5 x 450g jars

**5 Seville oranges, defrosted**
**2 lemons, plus the juice of 1 lemon**
**1 sweet orange**
**A good handful of lavender stalks and blossoms, rinsed**
**1 litre water**
**About 1.2kg granulated or preserving sugar**
**About 20 tiny lavender blossoms**

Scrub all the fruit and remove the stalks. Halve the Seville oranges and quarter the lemons and sweet orange. Juice the Sevilles, adding the pips and membranes to a muslin cloth placed over a bowl, then shave off any excess pith and add this to the muslin. Slice the peel and the lemon and orange quarters however finely you like it.

Add the lavender stalks to the muslin, keeping the blossoms for later. Tie up the muslin bag and put in the pan with the peel, juice and water. Leave to infuse for 24 hours.

The next day, simmer the fruit for 1–2 hours until soft, then remove from the heat, cover and leave to soak overnight.

Remove the muslin bag, squeeze into a bowl and set aside. Measure the pulp and add sugar in a ratio of 4:3 pulp:sugar to the pan, adding more sugar if you prefer.

Add the lemon juice and juice from the muslin bag to the pan, stir over low heat until the sugar is dissolved, then boil fast. Heat the oven to 150°C/130°C fan/Gas 2 and sterilise the jars for 15 minutes, and the lids for 5 minutes. When setting point is almost reached, at 105°C (or use the wrinkle test on page 9), add the lavender blossoms to the marmalade – they will turn from violet to crimson in the marmalade.

Let the marmalade settle off the heat for 15–20 minutes before pouring into the warm jars and adding lids to seal (see page 9).

# BAKED COCONUT CHICKEN WITH MARMALADE SAUCE

To make your own panko breadcrumbs, cut the crusts from about 5 slices of white bread, whizz them in a food processor, spread the crumbs out thinly on a baking sheet and bake in an oven set at 130°C/110°C fan/Gas 1 for 20–30 minutes until crisp but still pale; don't let them brown or burn. Cool completely before you use them.

Serves 4

**750g boneless, skinless free-range chicken breasts**
**60g plain flour**
**2 large eggs, beaten**
**100g panko breadcrumbs**
  **(see introduction for how to make your own)**
**100g unsweetened desiccated coconut**
**Olive oil, for frying**
**Salt and freshly ground black pepper**

**For the sauce**
**3 tbsp orange marmalade**
**2 tbsp Dijon or grainy mustard**
**1 tsp chilli paste**
**Juice of half an orange**

Heat the oven to 200°C/180°C fan/Gas 6 and line a baking sheet with baking parchment.

Put the chicken breasts between two sheets of cling film and bash them flat with a rolling pin, then cut each one in half, or to whatever size you like.

In three separate bowls, put the flour with some salt and pepper added, the beaten eggs and the panko and coconut mixed together.

Dip the chicken pieces in the flour and shake them to remove excess, dip them in egg and let the excess

run off, then roll them in the panko mixture.

Heat some olive oil in a frying pan until hot, then add the coated chicken pieces and fry them lightly for a couple of minutes on each side. Transfer them to the lined baking sheet and finish them off in the oven for 7–10 minutes.

Put the sauce ingredients into a jar and shake well. Use as a dipping sauce for the hot chicken.

Our mothers and grandmothers were forced to be inventive with food; they 'made do', eating the chicken that was about to go bad, preserving eggs in isinglass during the winter, storing fruit and vegetables on newspapers in the loft; bottling, pickling and preserving produce for the lean months. Go back another century and they would have made their own cordials, ketchups and sweets, their ink, shoe polish, soap and hairwash (from borax and olive oil). We have moved away from seasonal foods and can have anything we want all year round – and we are overstressed and overweight.

My mother was well ahead of the game in practical self-sufficiency and the organic movement, partly perhaps because she'd been in the Land

Army. In the Fifties and Sixties our weekly
shopping order at home in Kent consisted
of a small cardboard box containing soap
flakes, tea and coffee. Ok, maybe cheese and
sugar too. Everything else, and for a short
while even beer, was produced or made at
home. Admittedly, our mother was unusually
pragmatic about rearing animals for food, but it
was vital to her to know what you were eating
and whether the animals had had the best life.
I recall that we sat down for three meals a day
and there was no snacking, much as we longed
for white sliced bread and fizzy lemonade.

# CHEESECAKE WITH MARMALADE

Serves 12

**For the base**
240g digestive biscuits
140g butter, melted

**For the filling**
500g good-quality cream cheese
120g caster sugar
2 tbsp plain flour
1 tsp grated orange zest and 1 tbsp juice
1 tsp vanilla extract
2 eggs and 1 yolk, beaten
200ml sour cream
5 tbsp marmalade, any flavour
Squeeze of lemon juice

Heat the oven to 180°C/160°C fan/Gas 4. Grease the base of a springform cake tin, about 20cm, and line the tin with baking parchment, just turning the bottom edges up the sides of the tin. (You can use a loose-bottomed cake tin but it's a bit trickier to unmould the cheesecake at the end.)

Whizz the digestive biscuits in a food processor until crushed but not powder. Pour in the melted butter and process until well mixed. Spoon into the lined tin, using the base of a glass to press the biscuit layer down evenly. Bake in the oven for 15–20 minutes then stand it on a wire rack to cool. Turn the oven down to 120°C/100°C fan/Gas ½.

In a food mixer, beat the cream cheese and sugar together until smooth and well mixed. Add the flour, orange zest and juice, and vanilla extract. Add the eggs and yolk, beat them in well, then add the sour cream and mix until combined; do not overmix. Pour the mixture onto the biscuit base.

Place the tin on a baking tray and bake for 45–60 minutes, until just firm with not too much wobble. Turn the oven off and allow the cheesecake to cool in the oven, with the door slightly open.

Combine the marmalade and lemon juice in a small pan and heat gently. Strain, allow to cool slightly then pour over the top of the cooled cheesecake. Chill in the fridge for 1 hour before removing from the tin and serving.

AUTUMN

**W**hen the citrus harvest is yet to come, frozen oranges will add a burst of colour and a sharp reminder of the heady summer days that have just gone by. As the air begins to cool, the leaves slowly turn gold and the harvest season rolls in, it's time to head to the shops and farmers' markets for the finest ingredients to accompany your marmalade. And start to keep a look out for the new crop of Seville oranges…

SEPTEMBER

# DANISH HYBEN MARMELADE

**R**osehips will be out and ripening in the hedgerows from August onwards. The rose bushes have vicious thorns, so wear gloves and cover your arms while picking. This is not quick to make but rosehips are packed with vitamin C and foraging is always satisfying.

Makes about 3 small jars

**1kg rosehips, washed**
**About 1.6 litres water**
**1 lemon**
**1 orange**
**About 450–500g granulated or preserving sugar**

Top and tail the rosehips to remove the bristly bits, cut them in half and scrape out the seeds inside. It is fiddly and I find it easier to use a thumbnail than a spoon; the seeds are itchy and you don't want them in your marmalade. Put the seeds in a muslin bag.

When you have a panful of halved 'shrimps' – about 800g – put into a preserving pan and cover them with double the weight/volume of water.

**continued overleaf**

Juice the lemon and orange and add the juice to the pan. Scrape excess pith off the peels and add to the muslin bag with the pips. Cut the peel into thin strips and add to the pan, with the tied up muslin bag.

Simmer until soft, about 1 hour. Measure the pulp – it should be about 750ml by now – and add sugar in a ratio of 5:3 (so 450g sugar for 750ml pulp), and the rest of the lemon juice. Remove the muslin bag, squeezing it over the pan.

Boil until setting point is reached – 105°C on a thermometer, or using the wrinkle test (see page 9).

Remove from the heat and leave to stand for 10 minutes or so, then use the sterilising and sealing methods to finish (see page 9).

**Note:** You could save time and cook the rosehips whole, without the whole performance of removing the pips and tufts. Then you would need to strain the cooked pulp through a mouli, so it is smooth. I prefer it to have a bit of texture so I think it's worth the trouble of cutting and deseeding at the start.

# BACON OR SAUSAGE SANDWICHES

When I was at school, we were given chipolatas for breakfast that were just on the right side of burnt, and we always ate them with marmalade.

Serves 1

**3 slices of streaky smoked
  bacon or 3 chipolatas per person
2 slices of sourdough or
  wholemeal bread, or a section of baguette
English mustard
Good dark marmalade**

Cook the bacon until crisp or the sausages until well-browned; you don't want floppy bacon or pink sausages for this.

Toast the bread (or warm the baguette), unless it's very fresh and you're not toasting it. Spread one side with mustard and the other with a thin coat of marmalade. Butter is optional. Add the bacon or sausages and eat right away. No ketchup needed.

# LAMB SHANKS WITH MARMALADE

Serves 4

2 tbsp olive oil

4 lamb shanks

2 onions, sliced

3 carrots, sliced

3 celery sticks, chopped

2 garlic cloves, crushed with a little salt

30g butter

3 tbsp plain flour

300ml red wine

300ml stock or water

Pared zest of 1 Seville or sweet orange

A sprig of thyme

A small sprig of rosemary

2 bay leaves

3 tbsp marmalade

Salt and freshly ground black pepper

Heat the oven to 160°C/140°C fan/Gas 3.

Warm the oil over medium-high heat in a large frying pan, season the lamb and add to the pan. Brown all over in hot oil, then lift the shanks out into a casserole dish.

Brown the vegetables in the frying pan, then add the garlic and cook for a moment. Lift out the vegetables with a slotted spoon and add them to the lamb in the casserole. Add the butter to the frying pan and, when melted, stir in the flour. Cook for a minute then add the wine followed by the stock or water. Add the orange zest, herbs and marmalade and bring the mixture to the boil. Pour into the casserole around the lamb, cover the dish with a sheet of baking parchment, add the lid and cook in the oven for about 3 hours.

If the sauce is too thin, remove the shanks and thicken it by whisking in a buerre manié (30g each of plain flour and soft butter, mixed together on a plate with a knife to make a paste) over medium heat until thickened. Replace the shanks in the sauce and serve with potato and celeriac mash and some green vegetables.

Somewhere between their useful beginnings in Chinese medicine and their current place as the chief ingredient in British breakfast marmalade, bitter oranges enjoyed a spell in the courts of Europe as a must-have seasoning in Renaissance kitchens. Agostino Gallo, a Renaissance agronomist and author from Brescia, described the excellence of citrus fruits as invalid food, of how their flowers could be used in salads and drinks, the fruit for chutneys, liqueurs, focaccia and spiced breads.

Sour oranges featured in European kitchens long before anyone thought of marmalade. Bartolomeo Scappi, in the 16th century, was the first of the celebrity chefs, an artist who loved to invent, elaborate and astonish. Born in 1500 in northern Italy, he served in the kitchens of cardinals such

as Lorenzo Campeggio, then Pope Pius IV
and Pope Pius V. At the time when much of
the world's power and intellect was centred
on the papal courts, Scappi presided over
stupendously decadent feasts, creating visual
jokes and raising cookery to an art form. There
were spit-roast goslings and smoked pike
with cinnamon and saffron, miniature castles
containing live birds; monkey brains and parrot
tongues, sugar sculptures of Greek gods, meat
and dessert dishes placed alongside each
other: cockles with citrus peel, hare with sweet
pastries. Bitter oranges were widely used in his
kitchens for their flavour and for their digestive
benefits – for gravies and sauces and notably
in his tortoise pie (which also required a peak-
condition tortoise, nutmeg, saffron, cinnamon,
mint and onions).

In his definitive work, published in 1570, *L'Opera of Bartolomeo Scappi*, Scappi provides recipes for buffalo and guinea pig, bear, dormouse, porcupine, as well as didactic drawings of the perfectly arranged kitchen and necessary tools, and the sourness from the oranges provided that essential extra something to cows' udders roasted in breadcrumbs.

Alas for Scappi, the glorious period of sumptuous dining came to an end on the accession as Pope of Pius V, who, like Jane Austen's Mr Woodhouse, mostly enjoyed a plain boiled egg.

## CHILDHOOD MEMORIES

With endless soft fruit and berries in the garden there would be a flurry of bottling each autumn. One evening my mother stacked the bottom oven of the Aga with Kilner jars of apple purée and forgot about them. There was an explosion that night that split the oven door in half and spread glass and hot apple over every conceivable surface. Mercifully the dogs were sleeping in the boot room and not in their kitchen beds when the apple bomb went off. Decades later tiny smudges of apple could still be seen high up on the ceiling.

# JAFFA CAKES

If you are making these for children, slice each exactly in half to make 24 smaller ones.

Makes 12

**15g butter, for greasing**
**2–3 tbsp marmalade**
**60g caster sugar**
**1 egg, plus 1 yolk**
**70g plain flour**
**20g ground almonds**
**Grated zest of 1 small orange**
**100g dark chocolate (70% cocoa solids),**
  **broken into small pieces**

Heat the oven to 190°C/170°C fan/Gas 5 and butter a 12-hole muffin tin.

Heat the marmalade in a small pan until just boiling, then strain into a bowl and cool, reserving the pieces of peel.

Whisk the sugar, egg and yolk together until thick and creamy, using a balloon whisk or an electric hand-held whisk. Gently fold in the flour, ground almonds and orange zest. Spoon the mixture into the prepared tin, dividing it equally between the holes. Bake for 10 minutes until risen and pale brown. Leave the cakes to cool for a minute in the tin, then turn out onto a wire rack.

When cool, trim away a very thin slice from the top of each cake to create a flat top, and spread with a teaspoon of marmalade, keeping it just away from the edge.

Melt the chocolate in a heatproof bowl over a bowl of simmering water, making sure the bottom of the bowl isn't touching the water. When completely melted, remove from the heat and allow it to cool enough to thicken. Spoon carefully onto each cake and, when almost set, mark the tops using a fork and put a piece of reserved orange peel on top. Put the cakes in the fridge to set thoroughly.

OCTOBER

# CHOCOLATE AND ORANGE FRIDGE CAKE

I used to make this for my children when they were small. Also for grown-ups.

Serves 12–14

335g digestive biscuits
115g butter
50g golden granulated sugar
3 tbsp golden syrup
100g good-quality dark chocolate
  (70% cocoa solids), broken into pieces
30g candied Seville orange peel (see page 68),
  or rind from marmalade, chopped
25g flaked almonds (optional)

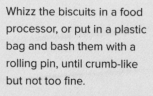

Whizz the biscuits in a food processor, or put in a plastic bag and bash them with a rolling pin, until crumb-like but not too fine.

Put the butter, sugar and syrup into a saucepan and add the chocolate. Melt on a low heat.

When you have a smooth mixture, mix in the crushed biscuits, orange peel or rind and flaked almonds, if using.

Spoon the mixture into a 18–20cm round baking tin, press down firmly with the base of a glass, and put it in the fridge until cold.

# CHAI MANDARIN MARMALADE

This is warming and delicious with many layers of flavour.

Makes 5–6 x 450g jars

3 Seville oranges
1 lemon, plus the juice
 of 1 extra lemon
6 mandarins or sweet citrus
 (or you could use grapefruit)
3 slices of fresh ginger, peeled
8 pink or black peppercorns
10 cardamom pods, bashed
½ tsp ground allspice
1 cinnamon stick
6 cloves
Good grating of nutmeg
2 litres water
About 800g granulated
 or preserving sugar

Wash the fruit, removing any stalks, then halve and juice them. Slice the peels finely, putting the pips and unwanted bits of skin and pith into a bowl lined with a muslin. Add all the spices and ginger to the bag and knot firmly or tie with string. Put the sliced peel and water into a preserving pan, add the muslin bag and leave to soak overnight.

The next day, bring to the boil and simmer gently for about 1½ hours, until the peel is soft. Remove from the heat and leave to infuse for another 24 hours, if possible.

Squeeze the muslin bag into the pan, and discard. Measure the cooked pulp and, for each 100ml, add 75g sugar. Add the lemon juice to the pan and cook over a low heat until the sugar is melted, then boil fast for about 20 minutes until it reaches setting point – 105°C on a thermometer, or use the wrinkle test (see page 9).

When the marmalade starts its boil, switch on your oven to 150°C/fan 130°C/Gas 2 and put a baking tray of clean jars, right way up, then use the sterilisation and sealing methods to complete (see page 9).

# VENISON WELLINGTON WITH PLUM AND MARMALADE SAUCE

Serves 6

600–700g trimmed venison fillet (loin)
1 tbsp olive oil
1 heaped tsp English mustard
25g butter
2 shallots, chopped
1 garlic clove, finely chopped
350g mushrooms, finely chopped
100ml white wine
1 tbsp fresh thyme, chopped
12 slices of prosciutto
1 x 375g packet of puff pastry
1 large egg, beaten
1 tsp poppy seeds (optional)
Salt and freshly ground black pepper

**For the plum sauce**
600g plums
30g butter
1 small shallot, chopped
1 garlic clove, chopped
1 tbsp fresh ginger
1 tbsp marmalade (ginger if possible; see
  page 91 for homemade)
1 tbsp light soy sauce

Pat the venison dry with kitchen paper and season well with salt and pepper. Heat the frying pan. Rub the olive oil on to the venison with your hands, place it gently on the pan and sear it on all sides so it's just browned. Remove to a plate, spread with the mustard and leave to cool.

Add the butter to the frying pan and, when melted, add the shallots and sweat over a low heat for a few minutes until soft. Add the garlic and cook for a minute or so. Add the mushrooms to the pan, increase the heat to medium and cook until the vegetables are almost a paste. Pour in the wine and cook down again, then add the thyme and set aside to cool.

Spread 2 or more overlapping sheets of cling film out on the work surface so you have a rectangle 40–50cm. Lay out the pieces of prosciutto, overlapping in a shingled pattern, and, using a spatula, spread the mushroom mixture smoothly over the ham. Place the venison fillet in the centre and, using the cling film, draw the layer of mushrooms and prosciutto up and around the meat. Roll it all up in the cling film, sealing it tightly, and tuck the ends under so you have a tight sausage-shaped roll. Chill in the fridge for 30 minutes.

On a floured board or surface, roll out the pastry to a rectangle of about 35 x 40cm and the thickness of a pound coin, big enough to entirely wrap the rolled-up fillet. Square off the edges and brush the surface with beaten egg.

continued overleaf

Carefully unwrap the mushroom-covered fillet from the cling film and place it at the edge of a long side of the pastry. Fold the pastry tightly around the meat, tucking the ends in as you go. Damp the final edge with cold water, pinching it to seal and pressing it down with the back of a fork. The venison should end up sitting on the pastry seam. Score the surface of the pastry a few times with a sharp knife; be careful not to cut right through to the meat.

Brush the pastry all over with beaten egg, scatter with poppy seeds, if using, and refrigerate for at least 30 minutes or up to 24 hours if you need to.

Heat the oven to 220°C/200°C fan/Gas 7 and put in a lightly oiled baking tray to heat up. Put the venison on the hot tray and bake for 30 minutes, until the pastry is golden brown, then leave it to rest for 10–15 minutes.

For the plum sauce, put the plums in a small saucepan with about a cup of water and simmer until soft and you can remove the stones. In another pan, melt the butter and cook the shallot and garlic until soft. Add the ginger, marmalade and soy sauce, along with the plums (strained if you like), then bring to the boil and season. If it's very thick, add a spoonful of water.

Serve the wellington with the plum sauce, and with braised red cabbage, steamed green beans or broccoli.

## QUINCE

**D**on't bite into a raw quince, whatever you do. Marmalade, as discussed on page 40, was historically made from quince, not oranges. These luscious-looking, golden pears, Cydonia oblonga, are in fact bitter, dry and bullet-hard. Many old-fashioned English gardens contain quince trees (the first recorded quince trees in England were planted at the Tower of London in 1275 by Edward I); they're not much valued now but make an outstanding rose-coloured jelly, or dulce de membrillo, a firm paste eaten with cheese (see page 164 for the recipe). It may have been a quince that so tempted Adam in the Garden of Eden: they are the Golden Apples of ancient legend, associated in Greece with Aphrodite and with love and fertility – often given to the bride (oddly not the bridegroom) at her wedding to sweeten her breath. They, like bitter oranges, were believed to assist both the digestion and the libido; prostitutes in 17th-century London were known as Marmalade Madames.

A 15th-century recipe for 'chardequince' involves cooking and straining quince, adding honey, eringo powder (made from candied roots of sea holly) and ginger, and packing the stiff paste into a round wooden box.

From the 16th century on, quinces were cooked and shaped into round wafers with designs or coats of arms imprinted on them by wooden moulds, prescribed by the apothecaries to aid the digestion. It's all a long way from the Women's Institute, where many people now buy their marmalade.

Now we mostly come across quince in the form of the Spanish dulce de membrillo (marmelada in Portugal) – in Argentina the same paste is often combined with cheese for a pudding called vigilante, and in Hungary there are walnuts in it. Quince are excellent cooked with pork or game, or added to apples or pears in puddings, turning ruby red and delicious with a heavenly scent. Given their old-fashioned and unloved reputation nowadays, people with ancient quince trees in their gardens often don't want them: next time you walk past a box of shabby-looking quince by the roadside or in the market, grab them with both hands.

# WHITE FISH WITH SEVILLE ORANGE HOLLANDAISE

Serves 4

4 fillets of any fresh white fish,
   such as cod, plaice or haddock

**For the hollandaise sauce**
**125g butter**
**3 egg yolks**
**½ tsp Dijon mustard**
**1 tsp white wine vinegar**
**1–2 tbsp Seville orange juice**
   **(from 1 orange)**
**Salt and freshly ground**
   **black pepper**
**A little butter, melted**

Melt the butter for the hollandaise in a pan over a low heat and pour into a jug, leaving the white solids behind and discarding them (this gives you clarified butter). Put the yolks, mustard, vinegar, orange juice and some seasoning in a blender or small food processor, and blend thoroughly. Leaving the motor running, pour the melted butter in a thin stream through the funnel. When the sauce is thoroughly mixed, transfer it to a heatproof, non-metallic bowl over a pan of boiling water, making sure the bottom of the bowl isn't touching the water, and stir until thickened and smooth. Remove the bowl from the heat, cover with cling film and keep warm.

Season the fish fillets, brush with butter and either grill for about 6 minutes each side, or bake in a 180°C/160°C fan/ Gas 4 oven for 15 minutes until just cooked and opaque.

Serve the fish with little new potatoes and broad beans or a green salad, with the sauce on the side.

# MARMALADE BREAD AND BUTTER PUDDING

Serves 8

8 slices of challah bread, crusts removed
50g butter, very soft
3 tbsp Seville orange marmalade
275ml whole milk
250ml double cream
3 large eggs
60g golden caster sugar
1 tsp vanilla extract
Grated zest of 1 orange
1 tbsp whisky
1 tbsp demerara sugar

Heat the oven to 165°C/145°C fan/Gas 3½.

Butter the bread slices on both sides and then spread one side of half of them with marmalade. Put together to make 4 sandwiches, then cut each into 4 triangles and arrange in an overlapping layer, almost standing up with the triangle point upwards, in a shallow baking dish, about 20 x 25cm.

In a large bowl, whisk together the milk, cream, eggs, caster sugar, vanilla extract, orange zest and whisky. Pour over the bread triangles.

Sprinkle the surface with the demerara sugar and bake at the top of the oven for 35–45 minutes until golden brown, puffed up and crunchy on top. Serve hot or warm, with single cream if you must.

# MEMBRILLO

Quince don't look that promising, but they smell wonderful when cooking. Membrillo is famously paired with Manchego cheese.

Makes about 1kg

**1kg quince (4–5 large fruit)**
**About 1kg granulated or preserving sugar**
**1 lemon**
**1 orange (Seville or sweet)**
**1 cinnamon stick**

Line a ceramic dish or ramekins with baking parchment. Wipe off the furry coating from the surface of the quince, then quarter, core and peel them. They are very hard and you will need a heavy knife and a swivel peeler. You can if you wish just wash them and chop them unpeeled, but they will be harder to push through a sieve later.

Pare 2 or 3 strips each of lemon and orange zest and juice the lemon. Put the prepared fruit, zest, lemon juice and cinnamon in a preserving pan and cover with water so the pieces of quince just float. Simmer for 30–40 minutes until soft, then remove the cinnamon stick.

Purée the fruit in a food processor, or push it through a mouli if you didn't peel and core the quince (or through a sieve if you don't have a mouli). There should be just enough water to make a purée, but if it's very stiff, like mashed potato, add a little more water. If you're feeling energetic, sieve it once more.

Measure the volume of pulp, return it to the pan and, for each 100ml of pulp, add 75g sugar. Stir over a low heat until the sugar is dissolved then turn the heat up high and cook for 45–60 minutes, stirring occasionally, until the mixture is really thick, has turned a deep red and rolls away from the side and bottom of the pan when you stir it. It should read 104°C on a sugar thermometer. Wear a surgical glove if you have one as it will make big gloopy bursting bubbles which will burn.

Spread the paste to a depth of about 3–4cm into the ceramic dish or ramekins. If you can turn your oven really low, to 120°C/100°C fan/ Gas ½, put the membrillo in for a couple of hours to dry out. If your oven will not go that low, turn it to its lowest setting and put the dishes of membrillo on the floor of the grill above the oven.

Cool then turn out and refrigerate. Cut into squares for eating with cheese. It will keep in the fridge for 3–6 months.

NOVEMBER

# PUMPKIN MARMALADE

Makes 3–4 x 450g jars

**1.5–2kg whole pumpkin**
**1 litre water**
**1 grapefruit**
**1 lemon**
**1 orange**
**80g fresh ginger, peeled and chopped**
**1kg granulated or preserving sugar**

Peel the pumpkin, remove all the seeds and fibres and roughly grate the flesh. Put into a preserving pan and add the water. Quarter all the fruits and remove any pips. Slice the quarters into shreds the size you prefer them and add these to the pan, with the ginger.

Bring to the boil and simmer for about 30 minutes until the peel is soft. Add the sugar and stir over a low heat until dissolved. Bring back to the boil and cook over a medium heat for a further 30 minutes, until the marmalade has thickened.

Leave to cool and settle for 20 minutes, then pour into warm sterilised jars and seal (see page 9).

# RUM MARMALADE

If I were making this marmalade in January or February with fresh Seville oranges and not frozen, I would replace the 2 lemons with another 2 Seville oranges.

Makes 4–5 x 450g jars

3 Seville oranges (about 400g in total),
  defrosted if frozen
1 sweet orange (about 250g)
2 lemons (about 200g in total),
  plus the juice of 1 lemon
2 litres water
About 1.5g granulated or preserving sugar
3 tbsp rum (I use Mount Gay)

Scrub and slice all the fruit as directed on page 32, reserving the pips, membranes and excess pith in a muslin bag. Put into a preserving pan, add the water and leave to soak overnight.

The next day, bring to the boil, loosely covered with foil, and simmer for about 2 hours until soft. Remove from the heat and leave to soak for another 24 hours, then remove the muslin bag and place in a strainer over a bowl; squeeze to extract all the pectin and add this back to the pan.

Wash and sterilise about 4–5 jars and lids in the oven at 150°C/130°C fan/Gas 2 (see page 9).

Measure the volume of pulp and add 75g sugar for each 100ml of pulp. Add the lemon juice and melt the sugar slowly over a low heat, then turn up heat and boil hard for 20–30 minutes until setting point is reached – either 105°C on a sugar thermometer or using the wrinkle test (see page 9).

Remove from the heat, stir in the rum and leave to settle in the pan for about 20 minutes before potting up, sealing with lids (see page 9) and leaving to cool.

# BAKED HAM WITH MARMALADE GLAZE

Serves 10

Large piece of smoked or unsmoked gammon,
  or raw ham, about 2.5kg
2 carrots, halved
1 onion, peeled and halved
1 celery stick
A few black peppercorns
2 bay leaves
1 orange, quartered
15 cloves
200ml ginger ale, tonic water or lager
4 tbsp marmalade
1 tbsp demerara sugar
1 tsp mustard

Soak the ham overnight if needed. Tip away the water and cover with fresh cold water and add the carrots, onion, celery, peppercorns, bay leaves and orange. Make sure the ham is covered with water and top up if required. Bring to the boil and simmer for 15–20 minutes for each 450g of ham, then remove from the heat. The ham can sit in its cooking liquid until you are ready to bake it.

Heat the oven to 190°C/170°C fan/Gas 5 and line a roasting tin with foil.

Remove the ham from the poaching liquid and place it in the roasting tin. Cut away and discard the thick rind from the top of the ham and use a small, sharp knife to slash a diamond pattern in the fat (making sure you don't cut down as far as the meat). Stud a clove in each crossover point.

Pour over the ginger ale or whichever liquid you're using. Warm the marmalade in a small pan, add the sugar and mustard and slowly pour the glaze over the ham. Bake for about 30 minutes, ensuring that the top doesn't burn.

# QUINCE JELLY

Lovely with game, ham or roast lamb,
or eat on hot toast.

Makes 3–4 x 450g jars

**1kg quince (4–5 large fruit)**
**4 long pared strips of orange zest**
**3 pared strips of lemon zest, and the juice of 1 lemon**
**15 pink peppercorns**
**1 cinnamon stick**
**About 900g preserving sugar**
**2 tsp rosewater (optional)**

Wipe off the furry coating from the surface of the quince then roughly chop them; don't bother to peel or core. They are very hard and you will need a sharp, heavy knife.

Put them in a preserving pan and add the zests, peppercorns and cinnamon. Cover with water so that they are just floating. Bring to the boil and simmer, partially covered, for about 1 hour.

Remove the zest strips, peppercorns and cinnamon stick and mash the quinces with a potato masher, just to break them down. Line a large bowl or pan with a muslin cloth or clean tea towel. Tip the quince and cooking liquid into the cloth, pick up the corners and tightly tie it into a bag using a long piece of string. (You can use a jelly bag for this if you have one, or even a clean pillow case.) Suspend the bag over a clean bowl to drip – I use the handles of a high kitchen cupboard to hang it from. Leave for 12–18 hours, squeezing every so often to remove all the juice.

Measure the volume of juice collected and pour into the cleaned out preserving pan. For each 100ml juice, add 75g sugar. Place the pan over a low heat and stir until the sugar is dissolved, then raise the heat and boil until it reaches setting point (105°C on a sugar thermometer, or use the wrinkle test on page 9).

Add the rosewater, if using, stir and pot up immediately into sterilised jars, adding the lids to seal (see page 9).

Scotland has a long history with marmalade. One of the first written manuscripts containing instructions for 'how to make orange marmelat' came from Helen, Countess of Sutherland, in 1683. This is a century before the legendary story of Janet Keiller buying a consignment of rotting oranges and inventing marmalade, though she may have been the first to add 'chips', or chunks of peel, to her mixture. It may also have been the Scots who first considered marmalade to be a breakfast food, rather than an after-dinner digestive comfit. Mackays are now the only producers of marmalade in Dundee, still making it in traditional copper pans.

When Dr Samuel Johnson visited the Highlands in 1773 with a young James Boswell, he was moved to pay a rare compliment: 'In the breakfast, a meal in which the Scots, whether of the lowlands or mountains must be confessed to excel us.

The tea and coffee are accompanied not only with butter but with honey, conserves, and marmalades. If an epicure could remove by a wish in quest of sensual gratification, wherever he had supped, he would breakfast in Scotland.'

This is the man who described oats, in his famous Dictionary, as 'a grain, which in England is generally given to horses, but in Scotland supports the people'. Marmalade continues to be a theme in his life: 'My wife has made marmalade of oranges for you,' writes James Boswell to Samuel Johnson in 1777. To which Dr Johnson replies:

'Tell Mrs. Boswell that I shall taste her marmalade cautiously at first. Timeo Danaos et dona ferentes. Beware, says the Italian proverb, of a reconciled enemy. But when I find it does me no harm, I shall then receive it and be thankful for it, as a pledge of firm, and, I hope, of unalterable kindness. She is, after all, a dear, dear lady…'

'MADAM— Though I am well enough pleased with the taste of sweetmeats, very little of the pleasure which I received at the arrival of your jar of marmalade arose from eating it. I received it as a token of friendship, as a proof of reconciliation, things much sweeter than sweetmeats, and upon this consideration I return you, dear Madam, my sincerest thanks.'

Even now we could do worse than give a jar of marmalade as a peace offering.

# ORANGE MACARONS

**T**hese are quick to make but it pays to be completely prepared, with all the ingredients measured and ready.

Makes 15

100g ground almonds
100g icing sugar
60g room-temperature egg whites (2 eggs)
¼ tsp cream of tartar
A few drops of orange food colouring
50g caster sugar

**For the filling**
90g unsalted butter, softened
45g icing sugar
A few drops of orange extract
A few drops of orange food colouring
1 heaped tbsp candied Seville orange peel
  (see page 68), chopped

Have ready a specialist macaron sheet, or a baking sheet lined with baking parchment. Mark out 30 circles, 4cm in diameter, leaving space between each.

You can do this by pencilling around the base of a herb jar or similar.

continued overleaf

Briefly whizz the ground almonds with the icing sugar in a food processor, then sift them into a large mixing bowl; don't force large pieces through the sieve and don't replace the wasted almonds, as the sifting process gives the right ratio.

Clean a separate bowl with a splash of vinegar and some kitchen paper. Whisk the egg whites until they form soft peaks. Add the cream of tartar and food colouring then slowly add the caster sugar and continue to whisk until the whites are stiff and glossy, and you can invert the bowl and the mixture doesn't fall out.

Fold in the almond mixture using a spatula. Taking special care, stir and fold to remove the large air bubbles, until the meringue is soft and ribbon-like, and streams slowly off the spatula.

Put a 1cm plain piping nozzle onto a piping bag and fold back the open end of the bag so that you can easily spoon in half of the mixture (standing the bag in a tall glass helps). Pipe small rounds of the mixture to fit into the marked out circles, holding the bag perpendicular and squeezing from the centre of each circle. Repeat with the remaining half of the mixture.

Tap the baking sheet a few times on the work surface to break air bubbles and settle the mixture, then leave to rest for 30–40 minutes. The surface should form a slight skin; opening the window helps. Heat the oven to 140°C/120°C fan/Gas 1 and check with a thermometer that your oven temperature is accurate.

Bake the macarons for about 16 minutes, opening the door briefly halfway through to

release steam. The macarons should be firm, slightly domed and have a ridged ring, or 'foot' around the base, like a small hovercraft.

Leave to cool completely on the baking sheet, then slide onto a wire rack.

To make the filling, cream the butter with the icing sugar and add the orange extract and orange colouring a drop at a time until you reach the desired colour. Stir in the candied peel. Pipe the filling onto half of the macarons, put the other half on top and twist lightly to make a sandwich. (Piping might seem unnecessary but if you try and spoon it on they may break.) Refrigerate. The macarons will taste better on the second day and will keep in the fridge for at least a week.

# MARMALADE TREACLE TART

Serves 8–10

6 slices of white or brown bread, crusts removed
2 tbsp marmalade
2 tbsp golden syrup
1 tbsp desiccated coconut (optional)
Grated zest and juice of 1 orange

**For the pastry**
225g plain flour
30g caster sugar
Pinch of salt
140g cold butter, diced
1 egg yolk
About 1½ tbsp ice-cold water

Put the bread in a food processor and whizz until you have even-sized crumbs. Remove and set aside.

To make the pastry, sift the flour into the clean processor and add the sugar, salt and butter. Process until you have a breadcrumb sort of mix, then add the egg yolk and, with the processor still running, just enough of the water to form a dough. Remove, loosely wrap in cling film and rest in the fridge for 30 minutes.

Roll out the pastry until large enough to line a round 18–20cm tart tin. Push the pastry well into the corners, and keep any spare bits of pastry.

Warm the marmalade and syrup together in a pan until runny, then add the breadcrumbs and coconut, if using, and let the mixture stand for a few minutes. Stir in the orange zest and juice then tip the mixture into the pastry case and spread it out evenly.

Heat the oven to 200°C/180°C fan/Gas 6.

Roll the leftover pastry into strips and lay them, twisting them as you go, into long lattices over the top. Damp the ends with water so they stick to the rim.

Cook in the oven for 10 minutes then turn the heat down to 180°C/160°C fan/Gas 4 and cook for another 15 minutes until nicely browned and well cooked. Serve warm with cream or ice cream.

# MARMALADE FRUIT CAKE

This is a light, everyday fruit cake, not a heavy Christmas-pudding type of cake.

Makes 12 slices

**450g self-raising flour**
**1 tsp ground ginger**
**Grating of nutmeg**
**½ tsp ground cinnamon**
**Pinch of salt**
**350g dried fruit and nuts: use any**
  **combination of raisins, sultanas, dried cranberries,**
  **candied orange peel, grated orange zest,**
  **crystallised ginger, walnut pieces**
**100g soft light brown sugar**
**150g caster sugar**
**3 eggs, plus 1 yolk, beaten**
**250ml milk**
**1 tbsp desiccated coconut (optional)**
**3 tbsp marmalade**
  **(more peel than syrup)**
**300g butter, softened**

Grease a 20cm cake tin and line with baking parchment. Heat the oven to 150°C/130°C fan/Gas 2.

Sift the flour into a bowl, add the spices and salt and mix. Put the dried fruit and nuts in another bowl, dust it with some of the flour mixture, and mix well.

Cream the butter and both sugars until smooth and fluffy, then add the beaten eggs a little at a time. If the mixture curdles, add a tablespoon of the flour mixture.

Stir in half the flour mixture and half the milk, then repeat. Stir in the dried fruit, nuts and coconut if using, and marmalade.

Pour the mixture into the prepared cake tin and smooth the top. Place in the centre of the oven and bake for 1½ hours, then cover the cake with baking parchment and bake for another 30 minutes. Test the cake by piercing it with a wooden skewer; if it comes away clean the cake is ready.

Let the cake sit in the tin for 10 minutes then turn it out and cool on a wire rack. It keeps well in an airtight tin for 2 weeks.

## ACKNOWLEDGEMENTS

**D**big thank you to my children Sophia, Drum, Rosie and Henry for all their marmalade-themed encouragement over the years (although Henry is doggedly loyal to chocolate spread), and for tasting and reading my stuff and consistently making the right noises.

I've loved working with the team at HQ, and I'm hugely grateful to Charlotte Mursell (now at Orion), for commissioning this book. To my editors Kate Fox and Nira Begum for their calm and unhassling help, and for not cutting out my jokes. To Sally Somers for her sterling cookery knowledge and unerring detection of my ingredient blunders: 'a tablespoon of nutmeg, really?' To Tamsin English for her eagle eye on the proofreading. A huge thanks to Steve Wells for interpreting the mood so well with the beautiful layout and design of the book.

NOTES

# NOTES

..............................................................................
..............................................................................
..............................................................................
..............................................................................
..............................................................................
..............................................................................
..............................................................................
..............................................................................
..............................................................................
..............................................................................
..............................................................................
..............................................................................
..............................................................................
..............................................................................

## NOTES

..............................................................................

..............................................................................

..............................................................................

..............................................................................

..............................................................................

..............................................................................

..............................................................................

..............................................................................

..............................................................................

..............................................................................

..............................................................................

..............................................................................

..............................................................................

..............................................................................

## NOTES

......................................................................................

......................................................................................

......................................................................................

......................................................................................

......................................................................................

......................................................................................

......................................................................................

......................................................................................

......................................................................................

......................................................................................

......................................................................................

......................................................................................

......................................................................................

......................................................................................

## NOTES

............................................................

............................................................

............................................................

............................................................

............................................................

............................................................

............................................................

............................................................

............................................................

............................................................

............................................................

............................................................

............................................................

**NOTES**

.......................................................................................

.......................................................................................

.......................................................................................

.......................................................................................

.......................................................................................

.......................................................................................

.......................................................................................

.......................................................................................

.......................................................................................

.......................................................................................

.......................................................................................

.......................................................................................

.......................................................................................

## NOTES

. . . . . . . . . . . . . . . . . . . . . . . . . . . . . . . . . . . . . . . . . . . . . . . . . . . . . . . . . . . . . . . . . . . . . . . . . . . . . . .

. . . . . . . . . . . . . . . . . . . . . . . . . . . . . . . . . . . . . . . . . . . . . . . . . . . . . . . . . . . . . . . . . . . . . . . . . . . . . . .

. . . . . . . . . . . . . . . . . . . . . . . . . . . . . . . . . . . . . . . . . . . . . . . . . . . . . . . . . . . . . . . . . . . . . . . . . . . . . . .

. . . . . . . . . . . . . . . . . . . . . . . . . . . . . . . . . . . . . . . . . . . . . . . . . . . . . . . . . . . . . . . . . . . . . . . . . . . . . . .

. . . . . . . . . . . . . . . . . . . . . . . . . . . . . . . . . . . . . . . . . . . . . . . . . . . . . . . . . . . . . . . . . . . . . . . . . . . . . . .

. . . . . . . . . . . . . . . . . . . . . . . . . . . . . . . . . . . . . . . . . . . . . . . . . . . . . . . . . . . . . . . . . . . . . . . . . . . . . . .

. . . . . . . . . . . . . . . . . . . . . . . . . . . . . . . . . . . . . . . . . . . . . . . . . . . . . . . . . . . . . . . . . . . . . . . . . . . . . . .

. . . . . . . . . . . . . . . . . . . . . . . . . . . . . . . . . . . . . . . . . . . . . . . . . . . . . . . . . . . . . . . . . . . . . . . . . . . . . . .

. . . . . . . . . . . . . . . . . . . . . . . . . . . . . . . . . . . . . . . . . . . . . . . . . . . . . . . . . . . . . . . . . . . . . . . . . . . . . . .

. . . . . . . . . . . . . . . . . . . . . . . . . . . . . . . . . . . . . . . . . . . . . . . . . . . . . . . . . . . . . . . . . . . . . . . . . . . . . . .

. . . . . . . . . . . . . . . . . . . . . . . . . . . . . . . . . . . . . . . . . . . . . . . . . . . . . . . . . . . . . . . . . . . . . . . . . . . . . . .

. . . . . . . . . . . . . . . . . . . . . . . . . . . . . . . . . . . . . . . . . . . . . . . . . . . . . . . . . . . . . . . . . . . . . . . . . . . . . . .

. . . . . . . . . . . . . . . . . . . . . . . . . . . . . . . . . . . . . . . . . . . . . . . . . . . . . . . . . . . . . . . . . . . . . . . . . . . . . . .

. . . . . . . . . . . . . . . . . . . . . . . . . . . . . . . . . . . . . . . . . . . . . . . . . . . . . . . . . . . . . . . . . . . . . . . . . . . . . . .